I highly recommend the Hou...
and have a better life. Sara ...
reflect how we are. She gently .... guided us through the steps
for change. The process that she has created is a thoughtful and perfect progression
of actions that have already changed my home but also the way I feel about it
and myself. Sara held a safe place for me to share my thoughts and feelings and
helped me to relate them back to my home. She encouraged me and gave me hope
with her kind wisdom and many ideas and techniques. M.P.

ৡৢৡৢ

HouseHeal took me to a place I could not have imagined prior to taking the course.
The tools given to me from each session are helpful and so positive in living all aspects
of life to the fullest. Our home is our small contribution to making the bigger world
a better place. I looked forward to each class with enthusiasm to share my new
awareness, to listen to the others' discoveries and to laugh and learn in a warm, loving
and non-judgmental environment. Thanks so very much Sara. P.M.

ৡৢৡৢ

I experience the change in perspective developed through your course daily.
D.S.

ৡৢৡৢ

My experiences throughout the course were life-changing and eye-opening. Wow!!
I feel like a whole new person, ready to welcome all the positive and happy
things (and people) into my life that I am destined to have. I am so grateful and
thankful for Sara coaching me through my challenges. My home will be a better
place to live in as I move forward, accepting the changes and inner peace that
come with real self-discovery. A.H.

ৡৢৡৢ

The content of your program is both amazing and wise. I now understand what
has been missing for me —the spiritual context for "de-cluttering". K.F.

ৡৢৡৢ

Motivational, inspirational, life-affirming and life-changing! Sara's passion,
dedication and love of the guiding principles take you to a journey of self-
discovery and oneness. S.B.

ৡৢৡৢ

I feel that I have been given the tools to make positive changes in my life now
and forever. K.P.

HouseHeal

HouseHeal

Transform Your Life through the Power of Home

With love,
Sara Brown Crowder

Sara Brown Crowder

BALBOA
PRESS

A DIVISION OF HAY HOUSE

Balboa Press books may be ordered through booksellers or by contacting:

Balboa Press
A Division of Hay House
1663 Liberty Drive
Bloomington, IN 47403
www.balboapress.com
1-(877) 407-4847

ISBN: 978-1-4525-4733-6 (sc)
ISBN: 978-1-4525-4734-3 (hc)
ISBN: 978-1-4525-4732-9 (e)

Library of Congress Control Number: 2012903033

Printed in the United States of America

Balboa Press rev. date: 3/5/2012

He is happiest, be he king or peasant,
who finds peace in his home.

-Johann von Goethe

For Jackson, my angel

*To my teachers, past, present and future, who
helped me to trust the healing power of unconditional love,*

*to you who read this book, for you will bring love and healing
not only to your own home, but to the world,*

*to my loving friends and family who believed in
what I was doing even before it took shape,*

to Gary, for your endless love and support,

thank you.

Table of Contents

Introduction

How HouseHeal Came to Be

HouseHeal emerged shortly after my husband Gary left a corporate executive job and became a realtor. Gary's real estate business grew quickly, and by his second year, I began going with him to consult with people on how to get their houses ready for market. I had been through two major home renovations, knew something about decorating, and was keen. I loved the house-prep work from the start and began working with Gary to prepare clients' properties for sale. I had a ball. I discovered gifts I didn't know I had.

From the very start, I was amazed that people allowed me into their homes in their raw, natural state. Clients trusted me with their largest financial asset and with their intimate personal space. I felt honored, and at the same time, I felt a huge sense of responsibility. For the first time in my life, I saw peoples' whole houses: closets, basements, and bedrooms *au naturel*. It was a privilege, and it was an eye-opener.

I was surprised by what I saw. In nice homes of lovely, intelligent people, more often than not, repairs and maintenance were not done. The decor was outdated and there was too much furniture and too much "stuff," as well as varying degrees of mess and dirt. Even in homes that were clean and tidy, often something was missing or "off" in the look and feel. I found that people were living in various levels of chaos or "stuckness." Because of all the books, magazine articles, and television shows about de-cluttering, organizing, decorating, renovating, and feng shui, I somehow expected that people would be on top of things. For the most part, they weren't. That was my first surprise.

My second surprise was how quickly a house could be transformed to get it ready for sale. With the incentive of getting more money for their property, people sprang into action. They rented storage lockers for their excess stuff, called junk-removal people, made trips to charity drop-offs, and painted whatever we recommended with whatever color we advised. They hung curtains, worked on the garden, put down new sod, put up new mailboxes, replaced outdated light fixtures, re-tiled floors, fixed broken windows—whatever was on the to-do list. One homeowner even cut the lawns of neighbors five doors in either direction and cleaned up graffiti in the nearby children's park!

Clients willingly and enthusiastically let us into their homes and move their furniture around. They allowed us to bring in our "staging" stock of furnishings and home accessories—throw pillows, rugs, bedding, towels, pictures, mirrors, lamps, tables, chairs—whatever was needed. Even if people resisted the changes at the beginning of the process, they jumped in when they saw the results and thought of the extra money they could get from the improvements.

It worked. The properties sold for excellent prices, often far beyond what the homeowners dared to hope. Clients raved about what we did to help them. They told us they wished they had made many of the changes and improvements earlier.

When people started to ask me to consult with them in their homes independently of the real estate business, I was thrilled and flattered. I loved the prep and thought that doing additional projects on my own with people who were *not* selling their houses would be the perfect fit. Then came my biggest surprise.

After only a few consultations, I realized that working with people who were not selling their houses was a totally different experience from prep. Rather than being a fun, creative, organized, adrenalin-pumping, time-sensitive, money-driven project, it was personal and emotional and there was no momentum. I discovered that when people were getting rid of stuff permanently, it was not the same as putting it into storage. I saw that choosing a paint color became a personal discussion rather than a professional decision—sometimes a very long discussion with no resulting decision! Even something as simple as recommending a new lamp could reveal a client's aversion to shopping or resistance to spending money. The fun disappeared very quickly.

Instead of simply advising people what to do and bringing in whatever "stuff" I needed for show, I now had to help them figure out what they wanted for themselves and nudge them to make decisions. I was part organizer, part decorator, part therapist, and part coach. It was a whole new world for me, and I didn't like it. It drained me. Not only that, but I didn't feel I was helping people in a way that would make a lasting difference to them. I knew people needed to have a stronger sense of what they wanted for themselves and learn to notice the details of their own homes without me having to point them out. I wanted to help people to make their home a place they felt good in, but I needed to find a new way to do it.

As a long-time self-help and healing enthusiast, I recognized that more was going on with people than what I saw in the house. It wasn't really about the house, at all. I knew that whatever was making people feel stuck, tired, frustrated, overwhelmed, discouraged, resigned, disconnected, or helpless in their house was present in other parts of their lives, too. If I was really going to be able to help people shift, I had to find a way to teach them to think for themselves, want things for themselves, and find their own power. I knew that simply having me or someone else consult with them or tell them what to do was not going to give them what they truly needed. It was going to take something deeper, something more powerful and personal. That's when the inspiration for HouseHeal came to me.

As you take yourself through the pages ahead, you will be inspired by a powerful new perspective on the connection between you and your home. I will show you not how to live in "show condition", which is for selling your home, but rather in what I call "Receiving Condition". When you live in Receiving Condition, your home supports you in "receiving" what you want to have and experience at home. You will learn the three keys essential to living in Receiving Condition that, once you understand them, will move you into action at home with ease. There are no rules for you to memorize, just principles, guidelines, ideas and examples to help you make changes in your life, step by step, beginning where you have the most influence: at home.

Part One:
You and Your Home

Chapter One
The Connection between You and Your Home

Some people say that your home reflects who you are.

Surprise! It doesn't.

Your home might reflect your taste, aspects of your character and personality, or your current circumstances, but it does not reflect *who you truly are*. It couldn't possibly. You are so much more than your home.

Your home says a lot, though, about *how* you are.

Your home and how you feel about yourself when you're there speak volumes about how connected you are to who you really are and how well you are taking care of yourself.

Look around the space in which you live. What do you see? What do you feel?

You and your home are connected energetically. What you see and feel in your home can tell you some important things about yourself right now.

The energetic connection between you and your home works something like this:

- If your home is filled with things you don't use, want, or need, your life will include things you don't want or need.
- If your home feels "not good enough" to you, you will feel "not good enough."
- If your house is a chronic mess, some aspect of your life will be a mess.

- If your house is in disrepair, some part of your life will be in disrepair.
- If your home feels overwhelming, your life will feel overwhelming.
- If your house is stuck in time, parts of your life will be stuck in time.
- If you can't relax and enjoy yourself at home, you won't be able to relax and enjoy your life.
- If you are concerned about what other people think of your home, you will be concerned about what people think of you.
- If your home looks perfect and beautiful but you feel no joy there, your life will look perfect on the outside but you will feel no joy inside.
- If you feel like you have no say in your house, you will feel like you have no say in your life.
- If you don't recognize and appreciate the good things in your home, you won't be able to recognize and appreciate the good things in your life.

And so on.

Before you start to analyze yourself or your house and jump into action, take a deep breath. It is important for you to understand the connection between you and your home and how it works. There is a lot more to it than you might think.

First, let's look at why your home is so important to your well-being.

If you want to love your life, feel good about yourself, and be genuinely happy, consider this question: How important is it for you to feel good where you live?

I hope you don't have to think too long on that one!

Whether you live in a mansion or in a tiny apartment, feeling good about yourself at home is vital to your overall well-being. Think about it. Your home is where you sleep, eat, and spend time with your family and friends. It's where you make love, read, listen to music, play with your pets, and take care of your body. It may also be where you work, write, or engage in creative projects. Your home is where you go for shelter and comfort when the rest of the world feels like too much. It's where you go to feel safe.

If you don't feel good about yourself at home, if you don't feel uplifted, supported, and loved at home, if you don't feel relaxed and comfortable and in control at home, what chance do you have anywhere else? No matter what personal or professional activities, relationships, or interests you have outside of your home, your home is your base, the foundation for your day-to-day living.

Now ask yourself: Where else in the world do you have as much choice and influence as in your own home? Everything in your home, including the people in it and your relationships with them, is what you have created for yourself. The look and comfort of your furniture, the feel of your sheets, the color of your dishes, the thickness of your towels, the art on your walls, the rugs on your floors, the clothes in your cupboards, and even the food in your refrigerator, are what you have chosen. What you do at home and how you spend your time there is your choice. You choose the people you invite in, the music you listen to, the books you read, the television you watch, the phone calls you make, the food you eat, and the websites you visit. You choose them all. Most important, you choose what you say, what you think, what you believe, and what you *feel* at home.

It's all your choice. Physically and energetically, your home is filled with what you have created, chosen, drawn to yourself, and allowed into your life. That's why your home and how you feel about yourself when you are there gives you more direct feedback about you than any other place in the world. And it's all within your direct influence and control.

How does it feel to know that you have influence and control in your home? Does it feel exciting? Or does it feel overwhelming? If you have that much influence and control, you might wonder why your home doesn't look and feel more like you want it to, especially if you have been intending to make changes.

How to create a beautiful home that supports living a life you love

I will guide you through a powerful process that will help you to see the degree to which what you experience at home is yours to choose. Through the details of your home, you can learn to recognize what you want and see how easy it can be for you to get it. Once you understand your natural ability to bring about changes at home, you will feel more confident to make all kinds of new choices for yourself, in every area of your life.

What do you think is stopping you?

You might think that you don't have the time, money, taste, power, ability, or energy to make changes at home. Think again! The best bumper sticker I ever saw said "Don't believe everything you think."

What you think and believe can keep you living in compromise, frustration, resignation, and disappointment. Wouldn't it be a lot more fun to live in creativity, self-expression, love, possibility—and action?

HouseHeal will teach you how to start loving your home and your life at a whole new level. If you can create a home that feels good, a home where you feel good about yourself, where you feel safe and can be your best self, it will serve you in every area of your life.

The HouseHeal process is simple, but you need to be ready. If you are ready, and apply what is here, you will be unstoppable.

Are you ready?

Let's begin.

Chapter Two
Show Condition vs. Receiving Condition

If you are selling your house and want to get the maximum return from your investment, you need to have it in *Show Condition*.

When you are living in a home and want to get the maximum return from your *life*, you need to have it in *Receiving Condition*.

Receiving Condition is just what it sounds like: having your home set up to support you in *receiving* what you want to experience in life. The focus of HouseHeal is to teach you how to create Receiving Condition in your home.

The easiest way to understand fully the concept of Receiving Condition is to look first at Show Condition and compare the two. It doesn't matter whether you plan to sell your home or even whether you own a home. Examining Show Condition first makes it easier to understand the deeper distinctions of Receiving Condition.

Show Condition

When I work with people to get their houses ready to sell, the goal is to create Show Condition. Location and current market conditions will always be the prime factors in the speed and price at which a property sells, but the look and feel of a house also plays a role, sometimes a big role, in the results. When I am preparing a house or condo for Show Condition, I have one goal: to make it as appealing as possible to potential buyers. There are two essential components to getting a home into Show Condition:

1. Minimizing
2. Beautifying

Minimizing to sell

Minimizing is what it sounds like: reducing your stuff to a reasonable level so that you can show off the space to prospective buyers. No house can look good when it is cluttered, crammed with furniture, or has clothes falling out of a closet. For a home to show its best to prospective buyers, it needs to be neat, clean, and organized. It is common for people to rent a storage locker (or several) just to hold what they remove from their homes to make them look good for "show." When it can get you more money for your house, you have a strong incentive to clear things out.

Minimizing also includes tucking away personal items and collectibles from view. Family photos, grooming items, or cute collectibles on display can distract prospective buyers who come to see your house, or even make them feel like they are snooping. Putting personal items away helps buyers feel comfortable while looking around and keeps them focused on the features of the property.

Here are some general guidelines for minimizing to sell:

- Remove furniture as needed throughout the house. Leave only the pieces that help to show off the size and function of each room.
- Clear kitchen and bathroom counters and other flat surfaces of papers and small items. This includes furniture such as coffee tables, side tables, dressers, and desks. Leave only a few well-chosen items on display.
- Organize any open shelving to allow "breathing room." Mix books with a few decorative items.
- Organize the insides of any built-in cupboards that people will open when they look at the house, in the kitchen and bathrooms, especially.
- Arrange closets so that coats and clothing hang easily. Remove unused hangers. Keep a portion of closet floors clear and visible.
- Clear all main floor areas except for furniture and lamps.
- Tuck papers away neatly in drawers or baskets.

There's a lot more to it, but you get the idea.

Beautifying to sell

Beautifying means making your house look ready to move in and enjoy, which includes decorating the space as nicely as possible, at a level that is appropriate for the house. Beautifying also includes making sure that everything is in good repair.

Here are some general guidelines for beautifying to sell:

- Check that interior paint is in good condition in a color that has general appeal.
- Add lighting as needed to make the space bright. Check that light fixtures are current in style and in good repair.
- Hang appealing artwork to accentuate the space. Use larger pieces of art where suitable.
- Use mirrors appropriately to reflect light and make the space feel bigger.
- Arrange furniture to show off the space.
- Make sure bedding and pillows look fresh and inviting.
- Make sure that floors and rugs are clean and in good repair.
- Update hardware on cupboards and drawers as needed, especially in the kitchen and bathrooms.
- Make sure that fixtures such as taps and towel bars are current.
- Check that shower curtains and towels are crisp and clean.
- Clean the kitchen to spotless, including drawers, cupboards, and appliances.
- Clean the bathrooms to pristine condition, including the insides of cupboards and drawers.
- Add or replace window coverings where needed. Light colors are generally better than dark, depending on the space.
- Make sure grass and gardens are in good condition and include comfortable outdoor seating where possible. If your home is a condo with a balcony or terrace, use planters.
- Check that outdoor surfaces (such as door frames and window trim) are in good condition and painted or stained as needed.
- Repair everything that is broken: drawers, door handles, missing trim, broken steps, holes in the plaster—every little detail.

And so on…

This may seem like a lot of work, but if you want to get top dollar for your house, it can be worth the effort. Buyers will be more drawn to a clean, tidy, bright home than to one that is out-of-style, cluttered, and dirty. It's that simple.

While your home is on the market, it's best to keep things as perfect as possible: kitchen counters clean and clear, bath towels neatly hanging on towel bars, toilet paper rolls full, lamp shades straightened, beds made, pillows fluffed, floors cleaned, and so on, right down to the last detail. Well-selected reading material on display can even give people the hope that if they move in they will have time to read good books!

Keeping a home in Show Condition demands extreme discipline. Show Condition is great for selling your house, but it is not a sustainable, healthy way to live.

It's surprisingly close, though. The optimal, healthy way to live is in Receiving Condition.

Receiving Condition

On the surface, Receiving Condition is remarkably similar to Show Condition. In fact, if you look at the description of minimizing and beautifying for Show Condition, pretty much everything on the list will benefit you even if you are not selling your house. It's not rocket science to figure out that a beautiful, clean home in good repair will support you in living a life that you love more than will a home that is cluttered, dirty, and in disrepair.

Still, there's a whole lot more to creating Receiving Condition. Cleaning, tidying and decorating will get your home into Show Condition, but it is not a guarantee that you will live in Receiving Condition. Receiving Condition goes far beyond how your house looks.

A home in Receiving Condition looks good *and* feels good. A home in Receiving Condition supports you in living life fully, happily, and with ease. A home in Receiving Condition helps you *receive* the experiences that you want in life on a daily basis. A home in Receiving Condition radiates with love and good-feeling energy.

Five Distinctions between Receiving Condition and Show Condition

As similar as Show Condition and Receiving Condition are on the surface, there are five key distinctions between the two that will help you to understand Receiving Condition better:

Distinction #1:
Show Condition is straightforward and physical.
Receiving Condition is complex and personal.

The goal of Show Condition is universal: to sell your house or condo for as much money as possible as quickly as possible. That's it. It can be a lot of work, but it's straightforward. If you brought in ten different people to give you an action plan to get your house into Show Condition, you might get some variations, but for the most part the advice would be similar.

Receiving Condition is far more personal. Receiving Condition requires that your living space support what is going on uniquely in your life and in your household. If you have ever worked with a designer or decorator, you know that before they give you ideas or recommendations, they spend time with you, ask questions, and get to know you. They ask about your likes and dislikes and the activities that are important to you and your family. They take the time to understand what you are trying to accomplish with your home.

To help clients achieve Show Condition, I don't need to ask questions about their personal tastes or their favorite activities. It's great when clients like what their house looks like in Show Condition, and of course they retain full say in what we do in their homes, but in the end it doesn't really matter whether Show Condition suits their tastes. All that is important is that we help them get the most money possible.

Receiving Condition, in contrast, is highly personal. The functioning components of a home in Receiving Condition are different for each person because they are based on individual needs, tastes, and interests.

Distinction #2:
Show Condition requires clearing things out of your **house**.
Receiving Condition requires clearing things out of your **life**.

To minimize for Show Condition, you can simply pack up whatever is not needed and put it somewhere else temporarily. To create Receiving Condition in your home, it is not enough to transfer your excess things to a storage unit. Receiving Condition requires that you deal with your stuff once and for all, and let go permanently of things you don't use, need, or want, and that do not actively support you in living a life you love.

If you have boxes, bins, or furniture stored in your friend's basement or your sister's garage, you stay energetically connected to those things. Whatever you still own remains in your energy field, whether it is in your home or not. If you have possessions lingering in storage, especially things that you do not miss, and that are not that important to your daily functioning and happiness, chances are those things are weighing you down without you even realizing it. I have an expression: *Out of sight, out of mind. Out of sight, still in vibe.*

Note: There may be circumstances where it makes sense for you to store things for a time, for example, when you are preparing your house for sale, undergoing renovations, traveling, or in a temporary personal situation. There may also be times when the size of your living space makes a small, long-term storage unit a logical, practical choice for storing items that you use and want to keep, such as seasonal decorations, sports equipment, or snow tires. Those are exceptions.

Distinction #3:
Show Condition is intended to appeal to **others**.
Receiving Condition is intended to please and support **you**.

Beautifying for Show Condition typically means making things in your home more neutral to achieve broader appeal to potential buyers. Show Condition helps other people imagine your home as theirs.

In contrast, beautifying for Receiving Condition is about creating a space that is beautiful for *you*, for your personal enjoyment and function. Colors, furnishings, fabrics, and finishes are yours to choose according to what feels good to you. Receiving Condition allows for far more self-expression and personalization in décor and detail than Show Condition.

Note: Even though beautifying for Receiving Condition is personal to you, true beauty is universal. You will find that when you create a truly beautiful and functional home from the heart, other people will feel good in the space, too, whether or not the décor is what they would choose for themselves. People recognize a home that is filled with love and beauty when they see it—and they feel it.

Distinction #4:
Show Condition, once achieved,
requires that everything stay as it is.
Receiving Condition, once achieved, requires continuous motion.

When your house is in Show Condition, the goal is to keep everything exactly as it is until the property sells. In Show Condition, ideally nothing changes from one day to the next. In fact, one of the challenges of living in Show Condition is the constant effort to keep things perfectly in place. It can be so stressful that people often move out for a time while their houses are on the market.

In contrast, Receiving Condition requires that everything in your home continuously change and evolve. A home in Receiving Condition feels alive, and that aliveness requires movement. In fact, if things in your home stay the same for too long, the energy will begin to stagnate, and you will start to feel it. Receiving Condition still calls for your home to be clean and tidy, but also ever changing. To keep a home in Receiving Condition, the energy needs to be moving and shifting ever higher. Energy movement in your home calls for daily attention to detail, along with ongoing changes and updates.

Creating Show Condition is a finite project. Creating Receiving Condition is an ongoing process.

Distinction #5:
Other people can create **Show Condition** for you.
Only you can create **Receiving Condition** for yourself.

The most important distinction between Show Condition and Receiving Condition is that only you can get your home into Receiving Condition.

For Show Condition, even if you don't know what to do, you can bring in professionals to manage the process of getting your house ready to sell from beginning to end. In fact, the professionals' job is often easier if you're not around! Achieving Show Condition is a lot of work and sometimes requires investing some money, but it is straightforward and can be delegated.

Only you can create Receiving Condition in your home. Even if you hire professionals to help with the process of organizing, decorating, repairing, renovating, cleaning, and tidying, ultimately you choose what is in your home. Other people can give you ideas, but you are responsible for the colors, finishes, materials, and use of space. You also manage the day-to-day care and maintenance of your home and the hundreds of details that go with it.

Most important of all, you create the feel of your home, its "energy." Your home's energy, at least a big part of it, comes from you. Your thoughts and emotions permeate your living space and determine much of what goes on in your home. You alone choose what you say, do, think, and feel in your home. You decide what you accept and what you tolerate in what's around you. Your personal thoughts, decisions, and actions outweigh anything that anyone else does in your home. Ultimately, the job of creating Receiving Condition in your home is yours and yours alone.

Note: Later, we will be talking more about the role of other people in your home, especially partners with whom you share money, personal space, and decision-making. For now, just focus on you and what *you* can do.

How Receiving Condition works in your home

Here is a simple image to help you to understand how Receiving Condition works.

Imagine a powerful energy force around you. Scientists are finding more and more ways to affirm and explain the role of this energy force in our world, but it is working in your life whether you are aware of it or not. For simplicity, let's call this energy force "the Universe."

Next, imagine that the Universe is ready and able to send you all you could wish for in this life, everything that you want to *receive*. Picture everything you want to experience, and feel it, just waiting for you. Think of what you would like to have—maybe a beautiful home, loving relationships, wonderful friends, flowing money, great work, fun, peace of mind, good health, travel, creative expression, leisure activities—whatever it is you want that money can and cannot buy. Think of everything you would like to "receive."

Now, imagine that the only thing standing between you and everything you want is the energy that you are sending out to the Universe. That's right, the energy that *you* are sending out. Your energy, and the energy of your home, is either *receptive* and is allowing things to come to you with ease, or it is *resistant* and is pushing away the things you want.

Picture what your life would be like if you could learn how to make your personal energy more *receptive* to what you want. Imagine everything you desire coming to you easily.

Your home is the perfect place for you to practice generating receptive energy or "good vibrations" in your life. The look and feel of your home plays a huge role in how *receptive* your personal energy is in allowing good things to come to you. As you begin to work with the details of your home, you will see the influence that you have on the experiences you *receive* in your life.

Think of your home as a traffic light to the Universe

A good way to look at this is to think of your home as a traffic light to the Universe. Your home gives off an energetic signal, just like a traffic light, either blocking, slowing down, or welcoming the experiences you want in your life: Red (stop), Yellow (stop or proceed with caution), or Green (go).

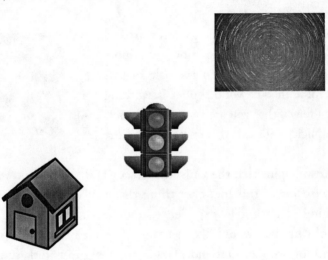

Think of where you live right now. What signal are you sending out to the Universe with the look and feel of your home? Is the signal Red, Yellow, or Green?

Everything is energy

Albert Einstein told us that everything is energy. When you learn to work with energy and start to notice the energetic vibration of what's around you, you can align the energy in your home to attract more of what you want to *receive* in life. In Receiving Condition, the energy of your home acts as a Green light to the Universe, helping you experience your life with more joy, love, and ease. The message of a home in Receiving Condition is: *"I am worthy and open to receive with love!"*

When you live in Receiving Condition, your bedroom supports good sleep, your bathroom supports daily self-care, your kitchen supports healthy eating, your living room supports good thought and conversation, and your dining room supports happy gatherings. If you have a home office, Receiving Condition supports you in being creative, productive, and prosperous in your work.

Most important, Receiving Condition culminates in loving relationships, beginning with the most important relationship in your life: your relationship with *you*. A home in Receiving Condition supports you in living a life that you love in every way.

How to create Receiving Condition in your home

Receiving Condition has three essential, sequential components that I call The 3 Keys: Awareness, Desire and Willingness. We will look at each key in detail. As you master The 3 Keys, something inside you will shift. You will begin to feel more confident and optimistic. Even when you get stuck, frustrated, or overwhelmed at home, as you will from time to time, you will know how to get yourself back to feeling good again, and know when it is the right time to take action. As you begin to notice the changes around you at home, bit by bit, you will start to recognize the depth of your own power to choose what is in your home and what is in your life. That's where creating Receiving Condition really gets fun and exciting.

Creating Receiving Condition in your home might sound like a lot of work. Sometimes it is. But it is work that becomes easy and natural as you follow the process in this book. Noticing the little differences in your day-by-day experience at home is at least half the fun. You will find that each step toward achieving Receiving Condition, even a tiny one, will make your life easier, often much easier.

This is an excellent time to take a break. We have covered a lot of material already, and more than likely you are processing these ideas on a deeper level than you even realize. Creating Receiving Condition is an intensely exciting and rewarding process, but it can also be emotional and overwhelming at times. Give yourself the chance to integrate what you have absorbed up to now.

Here are a few suggestions to help you:
- Go for a brisk 20-minute walk, breathing deeply, keeping your shoulders back and your head up as you walk.
- Deep-clean your kitchen for 30 minutes. Go looking for dirt.
- Do laundry. Iron.

- Detail the inside of your car.
- Sit quietly in your favorite chair and take deep, relaxing breaths.
- If you play a musical instrument, play your heart out.
- If you are an artist, paint.
- Sing. Dance.
- If you need to cry, let it out.
- Do something to help you assimilate what you have learned about Receiving Condition so far.

When you are ready for the next step, turn the page, and let's get started.

Part Two:

The 3 Keys to Living in Receiving Condition

Chapter Three
Key #1: Awareness

AWARENESS → *Desire* → *Willingness*

Awareness is the first key to creating a home you love and where you are happy.

The capacity for Awareness is in you. You were born with it. When you notice what is in your home, you have choice. If you don't notice what is in your home, you are powerless.

To live in Receiving Condition, you need to know what makes you and your home more *receptive* to the things you want in life. What will help you radiate a Green light to the Universe? Your home, with its hundreds of details, is the perfect place to expand your Awareness.

What kind of Awareness do you need for Receiving Condition?

Receiving Condition requires three basic kinds of Awareness:

1. Awareness of how your home looks and feels
2. Awareness of how "energy" works in your home
3. Awareness of your thoughts and feelings

Awareness of how your home looks and feels

Take a good look at where you are. Notice what you see. Begin slowly. Look at your bedroom. Look at your furniture, your windows and window coverings, your light fixture, your floors. Look at the light switch and the baseboards. Look at your bedding, your walls, and at what's beside your bed. Look at everything in your room, every detail from floor to ceiling. Just notice.

Next, look at your bathroom. How does your bathroom look and feel? How about the counter, the light fixtures, the mirror, the towel bars and the toilet paper holder? What about your bathtub, towels, bath mat, shower curtain, trashcan, and toilet brush? Look at colors, finishes, and accessories. How clean is your bathroom? Look closely at the floors, cupboards, walls, door and doorframe, sink, and taps. Look at every detail. Look at the personal products you have: soaps, shampoos, skin care, and so forth. Look in every drawer and cupboard. Just notice.

What about your kitchen? How does your kitchen look and feel? Look at your kitchen counters and what is on them. Look at your refrigerator and your stove, inside and out. What are your light fixtures like? How about your floor, cupboards, walls, sink, and taps? What does your kitchen look like? Just notice. How clean is your kitchen? When you open a cupboard or a drawer, look and see what's there. What do you notice when you look around you?

Practice a little bit every day, room by room, floors to ceilings, wall to wall, and notice what is there. What does your home look like? How does it feel?

As you develop your daily Awareness, refrain from evaluating what you see. Don't analyze. Just notice.

Write it down

It will help you to write down what you see in each room and how it feels. Not only will this help you deepen your Awareness, but making notes will provide a marker to help you to appreciate the progress you make as you move forward. It can be helpful to take pictures. Pictures help you to look at your space objectively.

Keep a healthy balance

As you expand your Awareness of how things around you look and feel, keep a healthy balance. If you are constantly trying to notice every little detail, you will drive yourself and everyone around you crazy. Depending on your starting point, you may be making big shifts in what you notice, so go easy on yourself. Just quietly and gently begin to notice what you like, what you don't like, what feels good, and what doesn't feel good. Whatever you see, start to feel excited about your expanding Awareness. Your personal power begins with Awareness!

A Healthy Awareness Balance

OBLIVIOUS ⇐	Aware/Intentional/Active	⇨ OBSESSIVE
(unhealthy)	(healthy)	(unhealthy)

Awareness of how energy works in your home

Awareness of energy is necessary to make any kind of meaningful change in your home. When we talk about the "energy" of your home, we are not talking about the heating or cooling system, but rather the feel or "vibration" of your home. Remember the Beach Boys' song "Good Vibrations?" If you have ever walked into a room after someone has had an argument there, you can feel it in the air. We all have the ability to sense the energy around us, consciously or unconsciously.

To understand how energy and vibration work in your home, think back to the image of your home as a traffic light to the Universe. Everything in your home, from your thoughts to your furniture, contributes to the vibration or the "energy signal" that you are giving out (Red, Yellow, or Green). Using your newly expanded Awareness of how your home looks and feels, consider the messages you are sending to the Universe. Each color zone carries a vibration with an underlying message.

Understanding and identifying a Red Zone

 A Red signal in your home is much like a red signal when you are driving. You are stopped. You might be able to look around, but you're not going anywhere. Even when you can make a legal right turn on a red light, successive right turns just keep you moving in circles. That is how it feels when you have Red Zones in your home: you feel like you are stuck or moving in circles.

Typical characteristics of a Red Zone in your home

- Chronically messy and/or dirty, piles of books or papers, boxes, clothes, or other things on the floor
- Too much stuff: over-stuffed closets, drawers, cupboards, or shelves; general clutter; often a predominance of inherited or "hand-me-down" items
- Lack of light; dark outdated window coverings
- Heavy or negative "vibe"—just doesn't feel good, residue of unhappy interactions in the space
- Lack of purpose, space not really used
- Disrepair: leaks, cracks, pieces missing, light bulbs burned out, hinges broken, things not working
- Awkward, worn-out, uncomfortable, or unstylish furniture
- Unattractive, outdated, or dreary décor, including light fixtures, hardware, cupboards, appliances, or worn-out flooring and carpets
- Predominance of unhealthy foods, such as soda pop, chips, cakes, candies
- Backlog of dirty laundry
- Too many electronics, cords, and wires, including noise (television, loud music, video games)

To learn from a Red Zone, understand that it is not merely what you see that matters. Your unconscious thought patterns or personal beliefs are being reflected to you in what you see. For example, with the common example of mess or dirt or clutter, it's not just the physical mess or dirt or clutter that is the issue, it's the vibration or message that the mess or dirt or clutter is sending to the Universe.

Red Zone messages

Red Zones in your home typically carry the energy of one or more of these statements:

- *I can't handle any more. I'm tired.*
- *This is just the way it is. This is just the way I am.*
- *I have no authority in my own home.*
- *I don't know what to do. I don't know what I want.*
- *I don't have enough time.*

- *I don't have enough money.*
- *I am at my limit. There's no room for anything more here.*
- *I don't care. My home is not important to me.*
- *My life is a mess.*
- *I deserve this. I'm a loser.*
- *I don't know why I live like this—it's too painful for me to think about it.*
- *I am not taking this on. Someone else should fix this.*
- *Life is hard.*

If you identify yourself with what's here, don't worry. We will look at ways to shift your Red Zones shortly. The most important thing to understand right now is that, however your home is, everything is all right. As you expand your Awareness, you will begin to see your power to change what is there, if you choose.

As when you are driving, a Red signal in your home carries a form of danger if you ignore it. It might not threaten your physical safety, although it could in some instances, but an unchecked Red Zone can compromise your emotional safety and your general well-being. And unlike a red signal when you are driving, a Red Zone in your home does not just eventually turn Green on its own. You need to take action to change it.

Understanding and identifying a Yellow Zone

 When you are driving, a yellow light is confusing. Do you treat it as a red light and stop or as a green light and accelerate through? Whatever you do, it feels uncertain. The same is true with a Yellow Zone in your home. It's hard to know what to do.

Typical characteristics of a Yellow Zone in your home

- It feels fine but not great, may be slightly dull or dreary, may have slightly too much stuff or even too little stuff
- Impersonal, neutral décor, perhaps even overly coordinated or trendy, like a decorator's showroom
- Reasonably clean, neat, and orderly, but doesn't feel inviting or comfortable; space may not be used much

- Lots of personal and family items on display, including inherited items
- Items feel as if they have been in the same place for a while, or alternatively, as if they are temporary
- Things don't look or feel quite right: pictures not hung quite right, furniture placement not quite right
- Something feels just a bit "off," as if something is missing

As with a Red Zone, it is important for you to understand the underlying energy of a Yellow Zone.

Yellow Zone messages

A Yellow Zone in your home typically carries the vibration of one or more of these statements:

- *This is safe, familiar, and good enough. This is all I want.*
- *I don't trust my personal taste. I don't want to embarrass myself by looking like I am actually trying. I don't know what more to do. I am afraid to go for what I really want.*
- *I don't believe I can have better than this.*
- *Leave me alone. I am doing fine. I don't need any help. I am holding it together, thank you. Don't push me.*
- *I don't have the time or the energy for more than this. I can't be bothered. Wanting more is simply too much work. This is as much as I am willing to do.*

Yellow Zones in your home can be tricky to identify because, on many levels, nothing is really wrong with them. If you have lots of Red Zones, you might call anything that is not in total chaos a Green Zone, when really it is more of a Yellow vibration. At the same time, people who are overly hard on themselves might designate an area as Yellow when its vibration might be more like a Green Zone.

There are no absolutes in identifying your color zones and, honestly, it doesn't matter so much what you call the zones as long as you raise your Awareness of what you have created around you. Be gentle and honest with yourself.

In your home, a Yellow Zone can carry the vibration of confusion and low-level stress, similar to the effect of a yellow traffic light. Even if you treat the yellow light as green and get through safely, you do not experience the same feeling of ease as you do with a true green light.

Understanding and identifying a Green Zone

 When you are driving, a green light allows you to move forward. You have the right of way. For safety, you still check to make sure that everyone else is following the rules and that you are safe, but you are free to move ahead. The same is true with a Green Zone in your home. A Green Zone in your home has movement and feels good.

Typical characteristics of a Green Zone in your home

- Clean and tidy, everything has a place
- Aesthetically pleasing, probably even beautiful
- Feels good, feels right, has an aliveness and peacefulness
- Furnishings, art, and other details work well together
- The space has a clear function and is used for its purpose
- Sufficient light and light can be adjusted
- Good, happy things happen in the space
- Comfortable and inviting
- People enjoy being in the space and gravitate there

Green Zone messages

As with the Red and Yellow Zones, the most important aspect of the Green Zone is the underlying energy signal it gives out.

A Green Zone typically carries the energy of one or more of these statements:

- *I accept responsibility for my life. I know that I create my own experience.*
- *I trust in an abundant Universe. Life is good.*
- *I know what I want and I am worthy of receiving it.*
- *I love being surrounded by beauty. I am confident in my own taste.*
- *I make time for what is most important to me.*
- *I choose what I allow into my home and my life.*
- *I welcome help.*
- *I treat myself and others with love and kindness.*

Just like getting a green light when you are driving, a Green vibration in your home brings a sense of ease. You still have to pay attention to detail, because a Green Zone in your home may turn Yellow or even Red over time. However, unlike a traffic light, with proper care and attention, the Green signal in your home has the potential to remain Green indefinitely.

Mapping the zones in your home

To identify the predominant energy signal that you are giving out to the Universe through your home, it is helpful to map out your color zones.

Draw a rough floor plan of your home

On a blank sheet of paper, draw a rough floor plan of where you live. It doesn't matter whether it is a house, condominium, apartment, or even just a room. The principles are the same, no matter where you live. If you have more than one level of living space, start with your primary living area and proceed floor by floor. If you have a basement, assess the basement area last, and separately.

Don't worry about getting your floor plan perfectly to scale. You don't have to be an architect to do this exercise. Just draw the outline of your space clearly enough so that you know what you are identifying.

Identify the color zones in your home

Your home will be a mix of color zones, sometimes even different color vibrations within the same room.

There is no right or wrong. This is just for you. Use your intuition.

- Scan each room in your mind, or, if you are at home while doing this exercise, you can look at the actual space.
- Notice how you feel as you walk through or scan the space in your mind.
- Look at what is there. Assess the feel and functionality of each space, as well as how it looks.
- What is your first instinct: Red, Yellow, or Green?

Mark the color zones on your floor plan

In workshops, I give people sticky colored dots to mark their zones. You can use markers, crayons, or whatever you have.

- Do your best to identify your color (energy) zones honestly. You won't help yourself if you are in denial about what is there, nor will you help yourself if you are overly critical. Remember, the goal here is to become aware of your starting point so that you can move forward from wherever you are.
- Consider the feel and functionality of the space as well as how it looks. Do good things happen here? Do you enjoy being here?
- Identify the zones for you, no matter who else is in your house. My husband and I frequently have differing perceptions of our home, and that's fine. This exercise is for you, as seen from your perspective.
- You do not need to defend or justify anything in your house. Just be willing to see and feel what is there for you.
- You can be specific. In one of my workshops, a person used a green dot to mark her new refrigerator because it brought her such pleasure. If there are specific things you love in your house, even if things you don't like surround them, go ahead and give them a green dot.

Do this assessment honestly and gently, without criticizing yourself or other people. This exercise is not a test or a contest. If you feel discouraged, overwhelmed, or experience anything that feels like a negative emotion, breathe in and let it go. The ultimate goal in all of this work is to help you know what you want, get into action, and make a change. If you follow the process here, it will be easier than you think, I promise. Your initial assessment of your home is just your starting point.

Optimal color percentages for achieving Receiving Condition

Once you have made your assessment of your living space, estimate as best you can the *total* percentage of each color in your home. If you have a basement, calculate it separately.

How much of your home is radiating the energy of Red, of Yellow, of Green?

Estimated current color percentages (above grade)

Red   _____%

Yellow   _____%

Green   _____%

Total   100%

If you have a basement area or live in a basement apartment, calculate separately:

Red   _____%

Yellow   _____%

Green   _____%

Total   100%

Now let's look at the *optimal* percentages needed to create the vibration of Receiving Condition in your living space. Remember, these percentages are guidelines to serve your ultimate goal. *These percentages apply to above-grade living space only, not including your basement area.*

What do you think is the optimal *minimum* percentage of Green in your total living space needed for you to live in Receiving Condition? _____

What do you think is the optimal *maximum* percentage of Yellow in your total living space needed for you to live in Receiving Condition? _____

What do you think is the optimal *maximum* percentage of Red in your total living space that will allow you to live in Receiving Condition? _____

If you have a basement in your home

What do you think is the optimal *maximum* percentage of Red for your basement to be in Receiving Condition? _____

What do you think is the optimal *minimum* percentage of Green for your basement to be in Receiving Condition? _____

Are you ready for the answers?

Remember, these numbers are meant to serve as a guideline and incentive, not as a test to pass or fail. Wherever you are starting from is fine.

The optimal *minimum* percentage of Green in your total living space that is needed for you to live in Receiving Condition is 70–75%.

The optimal *maximum* percentage of Yellow in your total living space that is needed for you to live in Receiving Condition is 15–25%.

The optimal *maximum* percentage of Red in your total living space that is needed for you to live in Receiving Condition is 5–10 %.

Basement area

For the basement area of your home, the optimal *minimum* percentage of Green is zero. That's right, zero. Green is not required in a basement. Before you get too excited, consider that the optimal *maximum* percentage of Red is also zero. Basement areas are fine when they are Yellow in vibration.

Your above-grade living space is the space most important to your well-being. Your first priority is to focus on raising the vibration of your main living space. As your main living space becomes more beautiful and "Green," you will find it easier to deal with whatever is lurking in your basement.

If you live in a basement apartment

Make an extra effort to eliminate Red Zones as quickly as possible, and try to create as many Green Zones as you can. As you do that, more than likely you will find yourself living above-ground before too long!

Keep in mind

These percentages are goals to work toward at higher and higher levels over your lifetime. Every home has zones of each color, but in terms of vibration, one color will predominate. Any upward shift you can make in the vibration of your home, even a tiny shift, will translate into a *big* difference in how your home feels. Even one drawer, one shift in attitude, one shelf, one thought, one closet, one conversation, one bin, or one small repair helps. Every little bit counts—a lot.

Remember, your identification of your color zones is the result of your personal interpretation. As you shift your personal energy vibration and your perspective, what feels like Green to you now can feel like Yellow very quickly, and vice versa. As you become more aware, your perception and your assessment of your space will change.

At this point, all you are looking for is Awareness. If you identify that you live in a partially or predominantly Red or Yellow Zone, you are simply being given the opportunity to see how the "energy" you have been giving out has been limiting the good things that can come to you. And you can change that.

Awareness of your thoughts and feelings

The third kind of Awareness that you will need for Receiving Condition is awareness of your own thoughts and feelings. Have you heard the old question, "What's the difference between an optimist and a pessimist?" The optimist wakes up and says, "Good morning, God!" and the pessimist wakes up and says, "Good God, morning!" If you were to listen to your own thoughts throughout the day, do you think you would be more like the optimist or the pessimist?

Beyond what is in your home physically, your thoughts and emotions contribute hugely to your home's energy signal to the Universe. Slowly and gently, begin to notice your thoughts.

You are the master of your thoughts

Whether you realize it already or not, you choose your thoughts. Tens of thousands of them every day.

There is no better place to practice developing your Awareness of your thoughts than right in your own home. Look around your house. Listen to your thoughts. Write down what you hear yourself think:

_____

_____

_____

_____

_____

_____

_____

You are not your house

Recently, my husband and I were going over a list of recommendations with clients, a couple who were getting their house ready for sale. As the list of recommended repairs and updates grew, the husband pleaded, "We're good people, really!" We all laughed, but it showed me how easy it is to take your home's to-do list as evidence of a personal shortfall. Catch yourself if you start to do that.

When you look around your home, you may see a lot of things that you would like to change. Be easy on yourself. Increasing your Awareness is not intended to create self-judgment or self-criticism, but simply to allow you to notice where you are. You will be able to tell if you are judging yourself by how you feel. Judging yourself or others deflates you; non-judgment uplifts you.

Remember, a home that is "stuck" is not a reflection of *who* you are; it is a reflection of *how* you are. A home that is "stuck" merely tells you that there is room for you to be more aware and pro-active in your life. I guarantee that once you begin to notice your thoughts, you will see that you criticize yourself far more than you realize. We all do. And we need to stop. Self-criticism is self-abuse. When you criticize yourself, you hurt your soul. Self-criticism sucks the life out of you.

Learn to fill your home with kind and encouraging thoughts about yourself and others.

Develop the habit of encouraging yourself

Listen to what you say to yourself in the continuous, half-unconscious voice in your head. Encourage yourself. For example, if you notice that your bedroom is messy, simply notice that it is a mess. If you feel overwhelmed by the mess, say something to yourself to help you feel better. For example:

"This room is a mess, but it doesn't have to stay this way. Step-by-step, I can do it. Easy does it."

Being good to yourself—the heart of living in Receiving Condition

To live in Receiving Condition, you need to vibrate with the energy that conveys, "I am worthy to receive." You cannot feel worthy while harboring critical thoughts about yourself. It is simply not possible. Releasing self-criticism and self-judgment is a key part of developing healthy Awareness. When you are able to look at the things you want to change in your home without going into self-criticism or overwhelm, you will have made a huge step forward.

> *"Simple kindness to one's self and all that lives is the most powerful transformational force of all."*
> —David R. Hawkins, M.D., *Power vs. Force*

Learn to notice how things feel

If you are inclined to think a lot, you may notice some resistance to feeling. Try to get comfortable with being in your body instead of your head, even if for only a minute or two.

If you are like I am and are naturally a "feeler," simply practice becoming more aware of how you feel. Whether you are naturally a feeler or a thinker, it is much easier to notice how you feel if you are grounded and connected. Being grounded in body means just what it does in electrical terms: connected to the earth. It is just as unsafe for you to be ungrounded in your body as it is for your electrical connections to be ungrounded. If you are not connected and grounded, your energy will scatter, and you will be at much greater risk of having an accident, making a bad decision, or being unproductive.

- Being connected and grounded is not something "spiritual" or "woo-woo."
- Being connected and grounded is necessary for your emotional well-being.
- Being connected and grounded is essential for your physical safety.

Learn to connect and ground yourself every day. It takes only a few minutes.

Exercise for grounding and connecting

Take a few minutes right now. Begin by noticing how you feel. Notice your thoughts. Notice how your body feels. Relax and let everything go.

Take a slow, deep breath in. Then slowly breathe out. Again. Breathe in slowly, as deeply and comfortably as you can. Breathe out, slowly and fully. Again. Let your body and your mind relax. Feel your breath going deep within you and throughout your body. Breathe in. And out. As you breathe, feel yourself connecting down into the ground, like the roots of a tree, going deep, deeper, and deeper.

Continue to breathe deeply until you feel a connection to the Earth. Notice how it feels to be grounded. Now, keeping the Earth connection, feel the energy going up your body and out the top of your head, reaching up far above you. Continue breathing deeply. Once you feel a sense of connection above you, feel again the grounding connection below you at the same time, and then allow the two to merge.

Notice how it feels to be grounded and connected after even a minute or two. Learn to recognize that feeling. You can do this exercise anywhere.

Note: There are many exercises and meditations available to help you ground and connect. Use the simple method here or find one that works for you.

Remember to keep a balance

As you begin to expand your Awareness, you may go from being oblivious to your thoughts, feelings, and surroundings to obsessing about them. It's okay to obsess for a little while at the start, but then bring yourself back to somewhere in the middle. HouseHeal is intended to help you engage fully in the physical world and love your life, not to cause you to analyze and live in your head. When cultivating your new Awareness, keep a healthy balance by taking stock at *appropriate* times, not all the time.

Practice developing your Awareness in segments of just a minute or so, a few times a day, and then go about your business.

Thoughts and emotions carry energy

Your thoughts and emotions carry energy. Some emotions carry *receptive* energy and some emotions carry *resistant* energy. If your thoughts do not predominantly help you feel better, they are interfering with the good stuff in life that is trying to get to you.

To create Receiving Condition in your home, you want to be spending as much of your time as you can in thoughts that have a receptive vibration.

Examples of receptive emotions

- Eagerness
- Hopefulness
- Gratitude
- Love
- Excitement
- Joy
- Willingness
- Confidence
- Peacefulness

Examples of resistant emotions

- Fear
- Worry
- Anger
- Sadness
- Guilt
- Shame
- Blame
- Grief
- Despair
- Frustration
- Hurt
- Doubt
- Hate
- Envy
- Insecurity

Of course, many other possible feelings or emotions exist, but these give you the general idea. When you feel hopeful, grateful, or excited, your energy or vibration is consistent with *receiving*, with saying, "*Yes, please.*" When you feel doubt, worry, or frustration, your vibration is consistent with *resisting*, or pushing away what you want.

Ask yourself, "Am I creating a *receptive* vibration with this thought, or am I resisting?"

Learn from your resistance

Resistant emotions can give you clues to where you are holding on to emotional hurts and limiting beliefs. When you notice a resistant emotion, you can use it to help you recognize where you need to heal. Ask the Universe to show you what you need to release:

"I recognize that I am being shown something I need to learn. Please, Universe, help me to release whatever is creating resistance and blocking my energy. Help me to let this go and move forward."

A resistant emotion is a signal from the Universe, telling you that something you think or believe isn't true. If you can remember that the deepest truth feels good, feels right, you will be able shift your perspective more easily.

As simple as it sounds, changing your thoughts and beliefs can be one of the hardest things you will ever do. Many of your resistant thoughts have been with you for so long that you don't even recognize them as thoughts; to you, they are simply reality.

You are thinking all the time. You have thousands upon thousands of thoughts every day. That's why it's so important to notice how you feel. When you aren't aware, your thoughts can take you to some crazy places without you even realizing it. Developing Awareness of your thoughts can reduce your resistant "mind chatter."

Notice when a thought does not feel good and take your thoughts to what feels better. Consider that when a thought doesn't feel good, something about that thought is not true.

When you understand and accept that real truth feels good, you will start to benefit hugely from your expanded Awareness.

Notice your mind chatter at home

Here's an example of how your thoughts in your home might go if left unchecked:

This kitchen is a disaster. No matter what I do, it just gets messy again. It never ends. Dishes in the sink. Crumbs on the counter. Stuff everywhere. I hate it. I never get any time just to relax. I feel so tired. I can't stand it. Look at this. I don't know how much longer I can take it. I'd like to bomb this kitchen, anyway. It's so ugly.

I need a break. I need a vacation. I want to go away. I want to run away. I need more money if I'm going to run away. I thought I would have more money by now. What is the matter with me? I hate not having money. Why am I such a loser? I thought life would be easier by now. I hate always feeling under pressure. I'm exhausted. This sucks.

Result: Overwhelm, no action.

Here's how the same initial thoughts might go if you notice them and change them in time:

This kitchen is a disaster. No matter how hard I try to keep up, it just gets messy again. Dishes in the sink. Crumbs on the counter. Stuff everywhere. I hate it.

You catch yourself and notice where you are headed. You take a deep breath and then change your thoughts.

But then, it's the kitchen. I suppose that's normal. Not such a big surprise that it gets messy. It's definitely easier when I keep up with it. It really doesn't take that long to clean things up once I get at it. Maybe if I spend a few minutes right now I can at least get it back to being half-decent. It feels so good when the kitchen is clean. I love coming downstairs in the morning and having everything clean and tidy. It makes the day so much easier. This kitchen is old and kind of ugly, but until I get a new one, I might as well keep this one clean and enjoy it.

Result: Hope, optimism, and action.

Discernment vs judgment

As you expand your Awareness, learn to distinguish between *discernment* and *judgment*. Discernment says, "this is like this." Judgment says "this is like this, and it's bad and wrong." Discernment is wise and receptive; judgment is hard and resistant. Learn to notice the difference, so you can become more receptive in your thoughts. Discern.

Let go of perfectionism

No matter how loving or spiritual you become in this lifetime, you will always have a degree of resistant emotions. You will always have more to heal and release, believe me. I used to long to be "done." I thought there would be a magic moment when I was suddenly wise and strong and all healed. I finally realized that, even knowing well the principles I teach, I will be learning and growing for the rest of my life. Despite my years of "healing," my family and friends (and even some strangers!) can tell you that I still have my emotional outbursts and meltdowns from time to time. Thankfully, however, now they are fewer and briefer, with more and more space in between.

Just learn to catch yourself when you go off on a tangent of resistant thoughts and *gently* bring yourself back to a place of feeling better.

Awareness of your thoughts and emotions and their vibration plays a huge role in creating Receiving Condition in your home, because your thoughts and emotions shape your actions. We will talk more about getting into action later.

Unconscious Awareness

You do not want to obsess about measuring or evaluating your home. You want to live in your home and enjoy it! In fact, ultimately you want much of your Awareness to become unconscious and let this process flow naturally.

Unconscious Awareness is not an oxymoron. If you have learned to drive a car, you might recall the awkwardness when you started. You were aware of every detail of what you needed to do: checking your rear view mirror, keeping a safe distance between cars, watching your speed, getting to know the response of the brakes and the gas pedal, checking your blind spot over your shoulder, using the turn signal.

If you were still driving with the same level of conscious Awareness as when you started, your driving would be slow and awkward. Perhaps you know someone who still drives like that! If you are an experienced driver, you have probably noticed that a certain dimension of your driving has become familiar and automatic, to the point where you can sometimes arrive at your destination and barely remember the drive. As an experienced driver, you have a constant layer of unconscious Awareness that helps to keep you safe. The same principle applies to day-to-day living in your home. You want to keep a balanced, healthy level of both conscious and unconscious Awareness at all times.

What now?

You have started to cultivate the three kinds of healthy Awareness that you need in order to live in Receiving Condition. That is:

- You are aware of how things look and feel in your home.
- You know how energy and vibration work in your home through your Red, Yellow, and Green Zones, and you know how *receptive* energy in your home can enhance your life experience.
- You have started to notice your thoughts and emotions and are beginning to understand the role that your personal energy plays in creating Receiving Condition in your home.

What now? With your new Awareness, you might feel the urge to jump into action. Go ahead. Clean out some drawers. Go get some new bedding. Take a carload of things you no longer need to a local charity. Put your old couch from the basement at the curb. Paint your bedroom. Maybe you have already made some changes in your home since you started reading this book. When I gave draft copies of this book to people to read for feedback, I got responses like, "Sorry, I'm only on Chapter 2, but I've cleaned out three cupboards."

It's great if you are already in action. Just know that taking action in your house with just one of The 3 Keys in your hand will get you only so far towards Receiving Condition.

To make a big shift in your home's energy, there are two more keys you need to know about. The next key is Desire. As motivational speaker Les Brown says, "You've got to be hungry!" Clear Desire gives you context and purpose for the choices and decisions you make. Clear Desire gives you hope. It strengthens your commitment. Clear Desire gives you a happy place to go with your thoughts. Clear Desire moves you into meaningful, consistent action.

To clarify your Desire, you will need to explore one of the most difficult questions you will ever face:

What do you want?

Summary of Awareness

- Awareness of the first of The 3 Keys of Receiving Condition.
- Awareness is your *point of power*. When you are aware, you have choice. When you are not aware, you are powerless.
- Awareness helps you accept and understand that what you attract into your home and into your life matches your energy or "vibration."
- There are three basic kinds of Awareness required for Receiving Condition:
  1. Awareness of how your home looks and feels
  2. Awareness of how "energy" works in your home
  3. Awareness of your thoughts and feelings
- Your home acts like a traffic light to the Universe. When you identify the Red, Yellow and Green Zones in your home, you become aware of what your vibration is drawing to you, and you can choose to change it.
- Learn to recognize the thoughts and emotions underneath your Red, Yellow and Green Zones.
- To live in Receiving Condition you need to be aware of how things feel, and to notice how things feel, you need to be grounded and connected.
- Your thoughts and emotions carry either *receptive* energy or *resistant* energy, and contribute to your home's vibration. When you have Awareness you can notice where your thoughts and emotions are creating resistance.
- As you expand Awareness of your home, release judgment of "this is good" or "this is bad." Just notice what is.
- Keep a healthy balance between being oblivious and being obsessive.
- Awareness is the starting point. The next key essential to creating Receiving Condition is Desire.

> *"With awareness comes responsibility."*
> —Barbara Marx Hubbard

Chapter Four
Key #2: Desire

Awareness → DESIRE → Willingness

Once you have healthy Awareness, the second key is to have clear Desire. If you want to live in Receiving Condition, it makes sense for you to know what you want to receive, right?

Desire gives you context, focus, and purpose for everything you do. Minute by minute, hour by hour, and day by day, you make choices by the thousands. You decide what to eat, what to wear, what to do, and where to spend your time, energy, and money. Knowing what you want helps you to set priorities and make good choices. If your choices are consistent with your Desires, life feels good. If your choices are not consistent with your Desires, life doesn't feel so good. If you have no specific Desires, your life will be random. Having clear Desire allows you to set your compass.

Having clear Desire is at the heart of creating a home that supports you in living a life you love.

Even if you are feeling pretty good about your home and yourself right now, things in your life are always going to be changing, so you might as well line them up to change for the better!

Awareness comes before Desire in the process of creating Receiving Condition for a very good reason. Can you guess what the reason is? That's right—it's much easier to clarify your Desire if you are aware of how you feel. Desire has to feel good in order to pull you forward; it has to feel right. Feeling your Desire requires you to be honest with yourself and recognize what feels true to you. Awareness of how you feel helps you know what you really want.

What do you want?

It is a simple question, and yet it stops most of us in our tracks.

Many years ago, I took a "Mind Power" course that was my introduction to the power of thought. I remember sitting in the front row, taking meticulous detailed notes, soaking in everything I could. I knew that I was learning something powerful that would change my life.

On the last night of the course, the teacher stood at the front of the room and said, "There is one requirement for all of this to work." Looking right at me, he continued, "You have to know what you want." I slumped in my seat. I wanted to cry. I had no idea what I wanted. That's why I was taking the course. With the exception of a general goal of feeling deeply happy at some point in my life, I had no clue as to what I wanted. Suddenly, I realized that I had to get clear on my intentions; no one else could tell me what to want in my own life. I had to decide for myself or I was going nowhere.

I did some research and talked to people, got clear on what I wanted, and within a few months I was working in the field of meeting planning, work that I loved for almost twenty years.

What do you truly want?

Do you know what you want? What you really, truly, deeply want?

You would be amazed how many times I ask people this question in workshops and get an apologetic, "I don't know."

Knowing what you want is not always as easy as it sounds.

The thing is, you *do* know what you want. Somewhere inside, you know. You just have to learn to believe that you can have it.

If you are like most people, you have a general idea of what you want, even if you don't know the specific details. You probably want things in your life to flow. You probably want to feel good about yourself—to feel loved, appreciated, and connected to the world. You probably want to be happy, healthy, and full of life, and to spend time with people you love and have some fun. You probably want to have a sense of purpose, to be engaged in activities that interest you, to have money flowing, and maybe to have an adventure here or there. You probably want to feel confident, safe, and secure and just to be yourself.

I want all of that, and more, but the question for me, in all my searching, has always been how to get it. How do I translate feeling good about myself into the specific details of my life? How do I create the wonderful life I want in the midst of the crazy, busy, stressful, and sometimes-scary world I live in? Where do I start? What do I do?

And now, I know. At least I know one very simple, practical, powerful way to start: I can start, you can start, and anyone can start simply, slowly, and step-by-step, at home.

When I saw inside people's houses, I realized I had found the perfect context in which people can practice knowing what they want in life. What better place than home to work with the power of your own thoughts to create a life that you love? Once I made the connection between home and overall well-being, the HouseHeal teaching just rolled out of me. Everything I had been studying, practicing, and trusting for twenty years came together in an instant.

You decide what you want

The beautiful thing is that you choose for yourself what you want in your home. You can choose what makes sense to you and what feels right to *you*. You set your own standards. Don't worry about what other people think, or question whether what you want is possible. You decide.

If you are saying to yourself, "But I live with someone else—it's not up to me to decide alone," let that thought go. For now, we are talking about you. We will talk about other people later.

How to know what you want

"Yes" is a feeling. You don't find "yes" in your head. You find it in your body. I'm sure you have heard the expression, "Go with your gut." Even when it's important to think and do research, after all of your analysis, you will instinctively make an internal check on how you *feel* before making a decision. It's human instinct. See for yourself. The next time you are trying to decide what to eat, notice what you do. You look in the refrigerator or at the menu, scan the options in your mind, and then before you decide, you check with your body to see what *feels* right. You might feel it in your gut area, your chest, your shoulders, or even as a sensation in your face, but you will feel your "yes" somewhere. It might be only a split second, and it might be unconscious, but you do it. You go for the feeling.

When you are having an "off" day and are not grounded and connected, chances are even something as simple as choosing what to eat will leave you with something that you don't really enjoy. Make sure that you are grounded and connected (remember the exercise from earlier?) before you make even a simple choice like what to eat. Being "connected" will help you develop your practice of Awareness. You need to be able to recognize it when something inside you says "yes" and when something inside you says "no."

Learn to recognize what YES feels like! If you do not know what your "yes" feels like, you might as well make decisions with the spin of a roulette wheel. Develop the habit of asking yourself: "Does this feel good? Does this feel right?"

Exercise: what "yes" feels like

Take a few minutes, right now. Close your eyes. Take a deep breath in and then slowly breathe out. Again. Breathe in. And breathe out. Slowly. Ask yourself to feel what yes feels like. Think of a time when you made a decision that you knew absolutely was right. Feel it in your body. Think of another time when you just knew a decision was right and it felt good. Stay in that feeling for several seconds. Remember how that feels. That feeling will be your guide.

Desire must feel good to pull you forward

Desire has to feel right, or it will have no power. True Desire will speak to your emotions and your body more than to your head. You feel your Desires; you don't just think them. Desires can be broad or specific, immediate or long-term, but to have any pull or magnetism, they have to come from your heart. When I set a goal of being genuinely happy many years ago, I felt that it was the only thing that mattered to me. I didn't have a list of accomplishments or material goals that I needed to complete in order to be happy. I just wanted a feeling. That Desire, as general as it was, is what set me moving in the right direction.

To create movement in your life, Desire must be charged with receptive, good-feeling emotion.

If you are more comfortable with thinking your way through things rather than feeling your way through, don't worry. Even with all the "feeling", you will still have lots of opportunity to think and analyze! Thinking is important, too. There are times to think, times to feel, and times to take action. The trick is to know when to do what.

How honest are you with yourself?

Do you know when you are being honest with yourself? Really? You might be highly skilled at fooling yourself, without even knowing it. That's why Awareness comes before Desire in the process of creating a home and a life you love. When you are aware, you will know if something is what you truly want by how you feel when you think about it. If what you are thinking about is your true Desire, you will feel it in your body. It will feel right. It will feel real. It will feel good. Don't be afraid to be honest with yourself about what you really want.

How feeling your Desire connects to what's in your home

Your home is your private laboratory, your personal playground, giving you literally hundreds upon hundreds of opportunities to practice noticing what feels good and what doesn't. Your home can help you recognize what you like and want in your life.

Start with the small things

The process of recognizing what you want and drawing it to you is the same for a tea towel as it is for a house or any other "big" Desires. When you practice with the smaller details in your life, you will see tangible results and begin to trust the process. You will start to recognize what "yes" feels like in your body so that you can choose what you want in every area of your life—work, finances, relationships, and health. You will start to want more for yourself and become more confident in your ability to experience it. Start where you are comfortable.

Clarify your Desires using the details of your home

Your Desires may be non-material. Maybe what you want most of all is a certain feeling or experience. Even so, you will still benefit by noticing the physical details of what is around you and seeing what you might like to change, because that is part of the energy you live in.

Let's look at an example of how you can use the physical details of your home to help you become skilled and comfortable with the process of expanding and clarifying your Desires. Here is one very simple example, but you can apply this process to anything in your home:

Imagine you are walking through your living room. Out of the corner of your eye you notice the throw pillow on your couch. You've walked by your couch a thousand times, but today you stop and look. For the first time, you notice that your pillow is worn, faded, and has a stain on it. You see, too, that it's old-fashioned and a little too small to be either in style or comfortable. You realize suddenly and clearly that you do not like your pillow. You have new Awareness! Congratulations! You have new power to choose!

Now what do you do with your new Awareness and power to choose? Here are a few options for you to consider. Do you:

A. Throw the pillow on the ground and jump on it, yelling, "Stupid pillow, stupid pillow, stupid pillow!"

B. Get sad and frustrated because you don't have money to buy a new pillow

C. Decide to keep the pillow anyway because it was your grandmother's

D. Toss the pillow in the trash and go to the nearest home accessories store and buy whatever pillow is on sale

E. Toss the pillow in the trash, feel excited knowing that you have the power to choose a perfectly fabulous new pillow, and head out shopping

Which did you choose?

I hope you chose Option E, or at least Option D, which would be the second best choice. Choosing Option D will still help you move forward, but you will miss the core purpose of the exercise, which is for you to become skilled at knowing what you want. With Option E, you can expand your Awareness and clarify your Desire at the same time.

For the sake of this example, let's say you choose Option E. You decide to get a new pillow. You feel excited. You think about what you want your new pillow to be like. You sit on your couch and look around to help you imagine your new pillow.

Does your ideal new pillow need to be comfortable or simply decorative? What color would you like it to be—a light color or a dark color? Blue? Green? Purple? Black? Brown? Beige? Red? Pink? Yellow? A solid color or a patterned design? If you prefer a pattern, do you like floral or geometric? Natural fabric or synthetic? Smooth or textured? Maybe leather or suede? What shape and size of pillow would you prefer? Square, oblong, or round? What style? Classic or modern? Trendy or timeless?

Do you see how many times you get to practice clarifying what you like with just one pillow? When you look around at your options, you discover styles and colors of pillows that you didn't even know existed. Notice how you feel as you look around at your choices. Do you feel excited or frustrated? Encouraged or overwhelmed? What are you thinking?

If you notice emotional resistance

If you notice emotional resistance to this process, you will know that you have an emotional energy block to release. Just notice and know there is an opportunity for you to heal something within yourself. We will get to that with Key #3.

Do you see how this works? And that's with just one pillow! Think of how many opportunities you have around you at home!

Your home is the best place in the world to practice clarifying what you want. Your home presents you with hundreds upon hundreds of opportunities to make choices, like a simple yet important pillow, that are in your direct control and influence.

If you feel restricted because money appears to be in short supply right now, relax. You do not need to spend a penny right now to engage fully in the process of creating a home you love! Lack of money is a reflection of the energy you are sending out. As you shift your energy, money and everything else that you want will begin to flow to you more easily. Know that everything is fine. Really, it is.

It's time to put your Desires on paper

Writing down what you want gives power to your Desires. Writing out what you want helps you develop ideas and be specific.

You have space here to write notes in the pages that follow. If you prefer, you can use separate sheets of paper. Even better, if you have a notebook where you can do the exercises included here, you can use the same notebook to continue to write down ideas, observations, and inspirations as they come to you over the next few months. You can even add pictures of what you want.

Before you begin writing, take a few seconds to be aware of your breathing and make sure you are grounded and connected. If you're approaching this exercise from a "connected" place, writing down what you want will feel exciting, liberating, and affirming. It might feel a little scary or uncertain, but it will still feel possible, and good.

Are you feeling good? Feeling ready?

As you think about the questions here, write whatever comes to you in as much detail as you can. Pretend that you have a powerful genie by your side to grant your every wish.

As you write, don't try to rationalize or justify what you want or figure out how you're going to get it. If you catch yourself thinking, "How would I ever get the money for that?" or "Right, like that will ever happen," give yourself a gentle shake. Let it go. And keep writing.

Describe how you want your home to look and feel. Write down everything that comes to your mind using as many descriptive terms as you can. Go ahead. What's your dream?

I want my home to be:

_____

_____

_____

_____

_____

Keep writing until you have gotten every thought, idea, and feeling down on paper. Say thank you, and feel as if what you want has already materialized.

What do you want to happen in your home?

What do you want to be doing in your home? What kinds of activities do you want to be able to enjoy at home? Be specific.

"Relax" is not a specific answer. What do you want to do to relax? Where?

"Time with my kids" is not a specific answer. What do you want to do with your kids? Play games? What kinds of games? Watch movies? What kinds of movies? Cook? What would you like to cook? Listen to music?

What kind of music? Do crafts? What kinds of crafts? Read books? What kinds of books?

Maybe you would like to host a dinner party, dance, paint, write, knit, play guitar, play cards, have friends drop by, have a little romance, or sleep a little more. Write down whatever comes to you. Maybe you want to be able to work from home. With every activity you identify, try to be as clear and specific as possible. You are placing your order with the Universe!

Activities I want in my home:

_____
_____
_____
_____
_____
_____
_____
_____
_____
_____
_____
_____
_____
_____

If you feel resistant to doing this exercise, ask yourself where that resistance is coming from. What emotion or belief is getting in your way? Is it a belief that you are not worthy? A fear of being disappointed? A belief that life is hard? Are you trying too hard to be "realistic?" Explore what resistance is there for you, say thank you for the lesson, and let it go. Have fun with this.

> *"Whether you think that you can, or that
> you can't, you are usually right."*
> —Henry Ford

It's okay to want "things." Really. Years ago, I bought a book I had never heard of called *God Wants You to be Rich* just because I liked the title. It's true. You are meant to be rich. Life is meant to be rich. Material wealth alone does not bring happiness, but if you are already happy, money flowing into your life can bring you a whole lot of great choices and opportunities. And when you have more, especially when you are happy, you also have more to give.

Being open to receive starts with allowing yourself to think about what you want, even if it seems impossible right now. When you can have fun thinking about what you want, you will have made a breakthrough. Allow yourself to fantasize about what you would like. Be playful. Get into the details of your home and list what you want. If you're like me, you will discover things to want that you didn't even know were options.

When we were looking at kitchen sinks a number of years ago, I found out that you can buy a sink with a built-in soap dispenser. Maybe not a breakthrough discovery, but what a great idea, and one less thing on the counter! The things you list here can be small or big. I love to bathe and always dreamed of having a separate bathtub and shower. Now that we have it, I love it as much as I thought I would.

What would you like to have in your home? New hardwood floors? What kind? Light or dark? Maple, oak, or bamboo?

A comfy couch? What style, color, and fabric? Luxurious bedding? What pattern and color? What about new light fixtures? Dimmer switches on every light? A wood-burning fireplace? Maybe you prefer a gas fireplace? A walk-in closet? How big? What kind of shelving? Heated floors in your bathroom? Fresh flowers every week? A steam shower? Would you enjoy a big laundry room with a television screen and a folding area? Stereo speakers in every room? A sunroom? Original art on your walls? New dishes? Natural stone counters? A gas stove?

Maybe you've always wanted a beautiful teapot, chef-grade cookware, or beeswax candles. Maybe you would like new measuring spoons. Big things, little things—list them all.

Include only things that you really want, not what you think sounds good. Don't be embarrassed to put down something really small. Often the small things bring the greatest pleasure. Be as specific as you can. Make your list as long as you like. Get a separate notebook if you need it. Check in to make sure you feel good as you do this. And breathe.

Things I would love to have in my home are:

_____

_____

_____

_____

_____

_____

_____

_____

_____

_____

_____

_____

_____

_____

_____

_____

_____

_____

_____

_____

_____

_____

_____

_____

_____

_____

_____

Remember: Let go of trying to figure out how you will get these things! Practice feeling as though you already have what you are writing down. Feel excited every time you think of something for your list, because you are training yourself to know and attract what you want!

Don't worry if you have trouble coming up with ideas at first. As you begin to notice what is around you in more detail, ideas will come to you and your list of Desires will expand easily and naturally. Remember that wanting more does not mean that there is something wrong with what you have. Receiving Condition requires movement, so it is healthy and necessary for you to develop new, good-feeling Desires!

Your Personal Statement of Home

One of the most powerful things you can do to boost your Desire is to write a clear statement of how you want to live. This statement will guide you in shaping the details of your home. It will give you context and momentum and help you make choices that are consistent with what you want to create for yourself.

For an example, here is my own Personal Statement of Home. Put anything you want in your own statement. Use words and phrases that sound right and feel good to you.

Sara's Personal Statement of Home

My home is a warm and welcoming place, a place of love, beauty, and comfort. My home is both a place of happy gathering and a place of peace. My living space inspires playfulness, healthy living, celebration, and creative genius; it is a "feel-good" place that is evolving to ever more detailed luxury and beauty. Abundance and wealth flow into this home, supporting and inspiring me in living into my full, extraordinary, and joyous potential. My home is alive with love.

What is your Personal Statement of Home?

Now, what is your Personal Statement of Home? What do you claim for yourself?

Note: You may use any part of my statement that works for you, but think of your own personal desires of how you want your home to be. Make sure that when you read your statement, it feels like it is in your words and it moves you emotionally. The power of your statement is not just in the words, but in the feeling it sparks within you.

_____

_____

_____

_____

_____

_____

_____

_____

_____

What you want will change and grow

Your list of Desires will change and grow, especially once you really start doing this work and see how quickly things can change in your life.

In just the last year, the wish list in our house has been checked off more quickly than ever before. We rebuilt our front porch, installed all new windows and new eaves (gutters, if you are American), had brickwork done, got new quartz countertops and glass backsplash installed in the kitchen, added a custom linen cupboard upstairs and replaced the fireplace in the living room.

And guess what? We now have a whole new list that is longer than the one we had before! Is it discouraging to always have more to do? No! It's natural. It's exciting. It's fun.

You will always have new Desires. Remember, Receiving Condition calls for constant movement. If things in your home are the same for too long, you will feel stagnation set in.

If you are still having trouble getting clear about what you want, ask the Universe for clarity!

If you are having trouble getting specific with what you want, that's all right. Take your time. Don't force it. It will come. If you are really drawing a blank, ask for clarity. Ask the Universe to help you know what you want.

When my husband and I needed to choose backsplash for our kitchen, I went to showroom after showroom and brought home sample after sample. Some of the tiles looked fine, but nothing gave us a wow feeling. I was getting discouraged when I remembered that I could ask the Universe to help. The Universe responds to questions about the little details of life — even backsplash! Soon after that I was making a salad when some grated carrot dropped on to the kitchen counter. I looked at the carrot on the counter and suddenly I saw our backsplash dilemma solved. The orange color of the carrot looked stunning with our warm brown countertop. An orange backsplash! I went on line and found a tile store near our house that I had driven by a hundred times but never noticed. When I went to the showroom, not only did I find the perfect tile as soon as I walked in, but the owners had just unpacked the tile sample that morning. Had I arrived even a day earlier, they would not have had that tile in stock.

One more important question

In determining your Desires at home, there is one more important question: How do you want to feel at home? Receiving Condition is about how your home feels, but it is also about how you feel at home.

How do *you* want to feel at home?

_____

_____

_____

_____

_____

_____

_____

_____

_____

_____

_____

Note: This is an important exercise that can spark some emotions, and that's good. Take a few minutes to allow your thoughts and feelings to sink in.

Feel as though you already have what you want

When you write out your Desires, notice how you feel. If you feel disappointed or discouraged because you don't already have what's on your list, or if you feel doubtful that you will ever have it, you will send out a resistant vibration while doing the exercise. If your thoughts and feelings are consistent with your Desire, you will feel something like relief, excitement, or even just a gentle calm.

Ask for what you want as if you are ordering lunch

Ask for what you want in your home as if you are ordering lunch at a gourmet restaurant, with someone else picking up the tab. In that situation, you don't question whether what you order will come to you or not or how you are going to pay for it. You don't worry that your order is going to be lost in the kitchen. You don't keep checking with the server to see if he got your order right. You know that what you asked for is on its way to you, and you look forward to enjoying it. Learn to feel the same ease with your Desires for your home.

Getting what you want is easier than you think

I had an early lesson in how easily what you ask for can materialize. Many years ago, I was listening to a recording by Esther and Jerry Hicks about the Law of Attraction. The Abraham-Hicks teaching is now widely recognized, but at the time, it was relatively unknown. The cassette tape included an exercise called "The Place Mat Process." I followed the instructions and made two lists, side by side, on a blank sheet of paper. On one side of the paper, I listed what I was ready and able to do myself today. On the other side of the paper, I listed things that I wanted the Universe to look after for me.

At the time I did this exercise, I had no money and was in desperate need of a new computer. I did the exercise exactly as I heard it. I made a list of what I was able do (quite short) on my side of the paper, and on the Universe's side of the paper, I wrote that I wanted a new computer and printer with all the newest software. I even added a bonus note that I wanted someone to teach me how to use it all. As per the instructions, I threw away the piece of paper and let myself feel relieved that everything was looked after. I didn't think about it again until three days later when I got a phone call from someone I knew at Microsoft, asking me if I would be willing to participate in a small business makeover. I would be given a brand-new, state-of-the-art computer, printer, and all the latest software.

In exchange, I would agree to report on how the new technology helped me in my business. Oh, and they would provide me with a private tutor to come to my home and teach me how to use it all!

I didn't know if I was more excited about the computer or the fact that I had just gotten exactly what I asked for—fast and for free!

Not everything you ask for will come as easily or quickly as my computer did, but some things do come shockingly easily when you allow them to. I am certain that my request, sent with gratitude and relief, brought my computer to me. So, let go of trying to figure out "how" you are going to get what you ask for. Just ask, say thank you, and let it go!

The process I used was later included in the first Abraham-Hicks book, *Ask and It Is Given*. When I read the instructions in the book, I saw that the exercise is actually intended more for help with a to-do list than with a to-have list, but it still worked for me!

> *"For some people, miracles serve as evidence of God's existence. For Einstein it was the absence of miracles that reflected divine providence. The fact that the Cosmos is comprehensible, that it follows laws, is worthy of awe."*
> — Walter Isaacson, *Einstein: His Life and Universe*

Receiving Condition and the Law of Attraction

Much has been written about the Law of Attraction in recent years. If you already know of it, you may have recognized that a big component of creating Receiving Condition in your home is learning to work with the Law of Attraction.

If you are not yet familiar with it, here it is in a nutshell: Basically, the Law of Attraction asserts that you draw life experiences to you that match your energy or "vibration." Your vibration comes from your feelings and beliefs, your feelings and beliefs come from your thoughts, and since you choose your thoughts, you therefore have direct influence on your own life experience.

That is my simplified interpretation of a very powerful and complex law of the Universe, but that's basically it.

One of the most important things to understand about the Law of Attraction is that your thoughts are received and processed by the Universe as requests. To the Universe, if you are thinking about it, you want it. The Universe does not filter your thoughts on your behalf and say, "I know that what you are thinking about is not really what you want, so why don't I give you something better, instead." The Universe makes no such discernment. It simply responds to your energy, thinking and emotional vibration. Through your thoughts, you choose what the Universe responds to.

It's kind of neat, actually. The Universe respects you enough to allow you to choose what you want. It does not impose its will on you. The Universe knows that you have the power and freedom to create a wonderful life experience for yourself.

What are your thoughts really asking for?

Pay special attention to this part because it plays a big role in Receiving Condition. If you are feeling worried, hurt, disappointed, angry, or discouraged and stay in that emotion for very long, your emotional vibration is translated to the Universe as a request for more things to be disappointed and discouraged about. If you worry about money, your "energy" will match financial lack. And guess what? That's right—more money trouble. If you feel genuinely grateful for the good things in your life, your vibration invites more things for which to feel grateful. And so on. When you think about something while charging it with emotion, your thoughts translate to the Universe as "please give me more of this."

As you notice your thoughts, ask yourself, "Do I want more of how this thought feels?" Focus your thoughts on what you want and how you want to feel. Fantasize about what you want. Let yourself feel as though you already have it! Feeling as though what you want is already yours helps you change your energy and your point of attraction. It's magic! It's actually science, but it feels like magic!

Roy & Margaret's New Closet

Our house came with a large, sturdy, free-standing closet in the basement laundry room. We didn't need the closet and, in fact, it was in the way. For several years, we talked about getting rid of it but did nothing. One day while I was doing laundry, I was suddenly compelled to move the closet. I called to my husband, and we hauled the cupboard up the basement stairs, onto a dolly, and out to the curb, marveling at how easily we did it. I taped a sign to the cupboard: "Free – Take me home!"

Within minutes an older gentleman stopped and began roping the closet onto the roof of his small car. It was a slow, awkward process, but eventually I looked out the window and both the closet and the car were gone. Then I noticed a piece of paper stuck on our front screen door. It was the paper I had used for the free sign on the closet. On the back of the paper, in shaky handwriting, was written, "Thanks for the closet. Roy and Margaret." I had shivers up my spine. What had made me move that closet at that particular moment? I will never know for certain, but I wonder if Roy and Margaret said to each other at breakfast that morning, "I don't know how we would get one, but we sure could use a new closet."

Synchronicity shows up in life's little moments and details.

Feel "good enough" right now

As you develop your Desires, be sure that your "I want" is not vibrating with the energy of, "I want this and I don't have it, so therefore what I have is not good enough, and I am a failure." If you are holding the deep belief that you are not good enough, there is a risk that you will want to have more in order to be good enough. If you believe you are not good enough right now, whether you are consciously aware of that belief or not, no amount of material accomplishment will change that feeling.

If you learn nothing else through the process of creating Receiving Condition, know that you are good enough—right now. Say it out loud to yourself: "I am good enough. I am good enough. I am good enough." Really mean it.

You are good enough. Do you believe that? You don't have to do or have a thing in order to be good enough. You already are good enough. Choose what you want in your home and in your life for the pure pleasure and joy of it. Choose it because you want to and because it's fun and exciting. You do not have to qualify to be worthy to receive; you qualified on the day you were born.

Having Desire does not mean you are greedy

Wanting more is not the same as being greedy or ungrateful. Notice if you resist wanting more because it feels like you are being unappreciative for what you already have. Wanting more is about living your best, fullest, happiest life possible and delighting in the wonders of the world—as you choose.

There may be periods in your life when you are genuinely, completely happy with things in your home exactly as they are or times when you choose just to coast with things as they are for a while. Enjoy those times; they are precious and usually brief!

If you still don't know what you want

Relax. If you're finding it difficult to get clear about what you want, don't worry. In fact, worrying about not knowing what you want vibrates with the energy of, "I don't know what I want," and that vibration perpetuates your dilemma of not knowing what you want. Funny how that works, isn't it?

Sometimes, knowing what you want begins with acknowledging that you don't know what you want. If you can admit to yourself that you don't know what you want, you can do something about it.

Even just for a minute, feel as though you know exactly what you want. Close your eyes and let yourself feel inside the relief, joy, and excitement of knowing exactly what you want. The feeling in your body is the same, whether imagined or real. Feel how good it is to know what you want, even when you are faking it! If you are going to make stuff up, why not make up stuff that feels good?

If you're getting scared of your own thoughts

As you begin to recognize the power of your thoughts, it is easy to wonder what will happen if you accidentally think a negative thought or, worse, have a bunch of negative thoughts in a row before you catch yourself. Relax. The Universe responds to your overall vibration, not to your every thought.

When you find yourself in a stream of resistant thought, just gently bring yourself back to thinking about something, anything at all, that feels good. It is okay to think about what you don't want. In fact, thinking through what you don't want can be extremely helpful in clarifying what you *do* want. It's also okay to go off on a little tantrum in your head every once in a while —just don't stay there for long. Let it go and be easy on yourself.

Love overpowers fear

In his book *Power vs. Force: The Hidden Determinants of Human Behavior*, Dr. David R. Hawkins tells us:

"…a few loving thoughts during the course of the day more than counterbalance all of our negative thoughts."

Dr. Hawkins explains that a loving thought is more powerful than a fearful thought on an exponential scale that is hard for us even to comprehend. This isn't just Dr. Hawkins' opinion. His statement is based on more than two decades of careful research.

Isn't that good news? If you are concerned about your negative thoughts, just spend a few minutes a day steeped in loving thoughts, and you will balance things out! When you notice how much better it feels to think loving thoughts, chances are you will choose to spend a little more time there, anyway.

Time to do!

There is a time to think and a time to do. In fact, as important as your thoughts are to your well-being, a few minutes a day of focused, intentional thinking may be all you need to keep you moving in the right direction. Thinking too much or too hard can tire you out and get you nowhere. The goal is to shift your energy and raise your vibration. At some point, that requires action.

Start small

To get into action, begin with a small project in your house, even a tiny project. Find a task that you can complete in 15 minutes or less. It could be something as simple as cleaning out a drawer, pulling five items out of your closet for charity, or clearing your bathroom counter. You will find that even a small accomplishment can shift the energy around you and provide momentum. If you don't feel like a house project, go for a walk, stretch, dance, or just jump up and down!

Turbo-boost your Desire with gratitude

Gratitude dissolves fear. Gratitude invites possibility. Gratitude claims, "It is mine." Gratitude says, "Everything is all right." Listen to your words, both those in your head and those you say out loud, and integrate from-the-heart thankfulness into what you say.

Don't just say thank you, feel it

Saying the words *thank you* is not enough. You need to feel the words and really mean them. Sometimes, I feel such deep thanks that tears spontaneously well up in my eyes. It is an amazing, beautiful feeling.

When you are able to say thank you even before what you want has arrived in physical form, you will start to see real shifts around you. The feeling of "I have it!" becomes your point of attraction. As you learn to align your thought vibrations with what you want, you will experience what feel like miracles.

Notice your fears

As you think through what you want to have in your home, be prepared to experience fear. You will. Fear is the number-one energy block to getting what you want, and it is in all of us. Common fears are fear of failure, fear of being hurt, fear of being disappointed, fear of being rejected, fear of being abandoned, fear of not knowing what to do, fear of being unworthy, fear of change, fear of being embarrassed, and fear of being alone. And the biggest fear of all is the fear of not being good enough.

If you are sending out the vibration, "I don't deserve this," how can you attract what you want? When your fears are strong enough, they create resistance and get in the way of Receiving Condition. To give your Desires momentum, you will need to recognize and release your patterns of fear. We will look more at how to release your fears when we look at Willingness.

Desire is Key #2—what's next?

Having clear Desire is essential to living in Receiving Condition. When your Desire is strong enough, you will find the strength and creativity to get you through the bumps and obstacles you encounter. Without strong Desire, it is easy to slip into resignation or complacency, or even back to being oblivious.

With both Key #1, Awareness, and Key #2, Desire, you are well on your way to Receiving Condition. The third and final key is Willingness. Willingness is more than taking on the physical work of creating Receiving Condition; it is also taking on the inner emotional work needed to release resistance.

At this point, with what we have talked about so far, you probably already have a certain level of Willingness and are eager to get into action. Let's look at the kind of Willingness that can help you to change your home and your life beyond your wildest dreams.

Summary of Desire

- Expanding your Desire will help to keep the energy in your home moving and flowing. Movement is necessary to create Receiving Condition.
- To know what you truly want, you first need Awareness of how you feel. Your true Desires will feel good. They will feel possible.
- The practice of clarifying your Desires with everyday items at home teaches you to recognize and trust the process so that making bigger decisions about what you want becomes easier.
- Look beyond what you already know. Get out and have fun exploring what is available to you for your home in order to expand and clarify your Desires.
- If you don't know what you want, relax and take your time. Inspiration and clarity will come.
- Keep a pen and notebook handy so that you can write down ideas as they come to you. You don't need to figure out what you want all at once, and it wouldn't be nearly as much fun if you did. Inspiration comes in sparks and layers.
- When you think about what you want, notice how you feel. If you notice anything that feels like resistance, let it go. You undermine your own Desire when you harbor resistant or limiting thoughts and emotions.
- You do not need to figure out how you are going to get what you want. Send your "realistic" side on vacation and let the playful, optimistic, adventurous side of you take over.
- Whatever it is you want, feel in your body that it is already yours. Say thank you and mean it. How you feel is a key factor in your Desires becoming real.
- Know that you are worthy to receive. You always have been, and you always will be.
- Ongoing healthy Desire is what will inspire you to action.

Chapter Five
Key #3: Willingness

Awareness → Desire → WILLINGNESS

No matter how strong your Awareness and Desire, nothing much is going to change in your home until you have the Willingness to follow through. In fact, Awareness and Desire *without* Willingness can be frustrating, discouraging, or even depressing. But when you have Awareness, Desire, *and* Willingness, you will start to feel your personal power on a whole new level. You will quite literally open the door to a whole new world. You will start to see and feel things in your home begin to shift.

What Willingness requires from you

What do you think Willingness requires? Persistence? Determination? Self-discipline? Absolutely. At times. To some degree. But Willingness goes far beyond determination, persistence, and self-discipline. If Willingness were simply a matter of disciplined action, it would be much easier to get there.

Willingness calls for letting go of resistance, beginning with resistant thoughts. No amount of determination, self-discipline, or persistence will see you through unless you are willing to deal with underlying emotional blocks (energy blocks). If you are thinking resistant thoughts and feeling resistant emotions, you are creating resistance. If you are holding on to limiting beliefs about yourself (*I am unworthy, I am not able, I have no time, I have no money, I have no choice*), you are creating resistance. If you are holding on to limiting beliefs about the world (*it's a mess, it's cruel, it's unfair, it's rigged*) you are creating resistance. When you allow old emotional wounds to linger (and we all have them!), you are holding on to resistance.

What Willingness feels like

When you reach a state of true Willingness, you feel a sense of ease. You feel as if you already have what you want, long before it even gets to you. You begin to let go of worrying about what other people in your life are doing or not doing to support you because you know that what you experience in life is up to you.

When your thoughts wander off by themselves, they take you to happy places in your mind. Issues that would have stopped you in your tracks before feel manageable. You might not know how everything is going to work out, but you know that it will. When you get frustrated or upset, you recognize that something in your thinking needs to shift. You know that you have a choice as to how you respond to any situation. When you get stuck, you seek and welcome help to move forward.

> *"No problem can be solved from the same level of consciousness that created it."*
> —Albert Einstein

Once you have Awareness, Desire, and even the first sparks of Willingness, you can begin to take action in your home and engage in your life at a whole new level. The beauty of the process of Awareness, Desire, and Willingness is that, by the time you really get into action, you are ready, which means that it will be easier for you to make real progress.

Taking the next step into Willingness

Like Awareness and Desire, Willingness comes in layers. The first layer of Willingness is to see your home in a whole new way. I don't mean just looking around you as you did in the earlier section on Awareness. I mean that you are willing to recognize and acknowledge what is there, physically and emotionally.

Your energetic connection to your home

Remember, you and your home are energetically entwined. As either you or your home shifts in vibration, the other will follow, whether the vibration moves higher or lower. If you're having a struggle shifting one, then shift the other, bit by bit.

If your house feels hopelessly stuck in Red or Yellow Zones, sometimes the most helpful thing you can do is to raise your personal vibration. You can do this by working through your thoughts to get yourself to a place of feeling better *before* you take action. Raising your own vibration will help you deal more easily with whatever is in your house.

If you are feeling personally bogged down, give a little physical push at home. Even for a short time, focus on cleaning, purging, organizing, or decorating, and take a break from thinking. Most often you will find that action helps to shift your mood.

Shift one, then the other, step by step. If you try to shift yourself or your home too far without allowing the other to rise to a reasonable match in energy, you will feel resistance.

Are you Willing to look at your Red Zones?

It can be emotionally challenging to deal with what is in your home. When you can get to the underlying emotion or belief reflected in how your home is or how it feels to you, you can make changes that are good for you. Remember, your home does not reflect *who* you are, it reflects *how* you are and how well you are taking care of yourself.

To help you see how you are on a deeper level, let's go back to the analogy of your home as a traffic light to the Universe. Get out the sheet of paper where you mapped out the color zones in your home: Red, Yellow, and Green. Let's look at what your zones are telling you about *how* you are.

Look at where you have identified Red Zones and consider the possible emotional roots of those areas.

Red Zones: Possible emotional roots

Here are some of the emotional reasons that people live in predominantly Red Zones:

- Overwhelm, fatigue
- Fear (of failure, or responsibility)
- Anger at themselves or others
- Self-criticism, lack of self-esteem
- Apathy, not knowing any better, not knowing anything different, lack of desire for something better
- Sense of entitlement, belief that someone else should fix it
- Unwillingness to ask for help, belief that they will "get to it" themselves one day
- Embarrassment, not wanting anyone to know or see how they live
- Despair, grief, feeling helpless, sending a cry for help
- Hopelessness, resignation, lack of faith
- Unworthiness reflected in lack of boundaries, not knowing how to say no
- Disappointment in themselves and their lives
- Rebellion, opting out, refusing to acknowledge what is there
- Depression
- Protecting themselves emotionally—mess and chaos keep people away and provide an excuse for shutting out the world

If you have identified Red Zones for yourself, does anything here resonate with you? Often the emotional roots of Red Zones are so deep that they can be hard for the people with the Red Zones to recognize for themselves. If you have identified Red Zones in your home, you may or may not find it helpful to know the specific emotional root cause. Sometimes, it is better to heal without ever knowing the underlying "why." The important thing is to release the emotional pattern beneath the Red

Zone so that the behavior can change, which is why it often requires time and care to shift Red Zones.

Red Zone challenges

- Red Zones can feel so overwhelming that even when you genuinely try to make progress, you can get stuck very easily in the heavy energy that accompanies them.
- Red Zones often require Willingness to ask for help, paid or "volunteer".
- Red Zones usually build over a period of time, and need to be remedied over a period of time. There is no quick fix.

Don't worry, we are going to look at how to shift a Red Zone shortly. Even if the level of disorder in your home feels overwhelming to you, you will be amazed at how quickly you can make changes once you shift your thinking.

Are you Willing to look at your Yellow Zones?

If you have lots of Yellow Zones, don't be surprised if you feel some resistance to looking at *why* you have them. You might feel defensive or want to justify why things are fine the way they are. People with a lot of Yellow Zones are often resistant to change, which is part of how they ended up with so much Yellow vibration in their home in the first place. You also might have a tendency to be hard on yourself. Notice your response and remember that there is no judgment in any of this, and there is no pressure on you to do anything differently. You choose.

Yellow Zones: Possible emotional roots

Here are some of the emotional reasons that people live in predominantly Yellow Zones:

- Fear of change, trying to hold it together, coping, high need for the familiar
- High need for self-sufficiency, unwilling to ask for advice
- Self-doubt, lacking confidence in their own creative ability and taste

- Fear of failure, wanting more feels like it means that what they have isn't good enough, or keeping things as they are feels safer than risking failure at something better
- Sensitivity, taking things personally, thinking about change feels like criticism
- Complacency, lack of awareness
- Sense of self-importance, being too "busy"
- Having a pattern of being stuck by waiting for the "right" time, an all-or-nothing approach, resulting in little change
- Feeling they don't have permission from other people (living or dead) to make changes

It can be difficult to identify and hard to acknowledge Yellow Zones, especially if you have a lot of them. It is challenging because there is nothing obviously "wrong" with them. In a Yellow Zone, things are reasonably clean. Things are reasonably tidy. Things are generally okay. But if you are willing to look, if you are willing to be honest with yourself, especially as your Awareness expands and your Desires become clearer, you will acknowledge that something is missing for you. It's not that things are wrong or bad, it's just that they can be better.

To shift your Yellow Zones to Green, you need to raise your Awareness and amplify your Desire even more before you step into Willingness. If you don't notice or want anything more than what is already there, nothing will change.

If you decide that you want more (i.e., if you expand your Desire), shifting the vibration of a Yellow Zone in your home to Green can make a huge difference in how your home feels and in how *you* feel when you are there. Remember, Receiving Condition requires motion. Leaving things the same over time will bog down your energy, whether you notice it or not.

Yellow Zone challenges

- Yellow Zones breed complacency. It is easier to take the path of least resistance and leave things as they are when nothing is obviously wrong.
- Sometimes what are identified as Yellow Zones have energy that is more like a Red Zone and therefore are harder to change (and live in) than it might seem at first.

- A Yellow Zone can keep your Desires at a lower level. People often identify Yellow Zones as Green Zones because they have not experienced or imagined better for themselves.

At one of my workshops, I overheard a couple of participants chatting about how unnerving they found Yellow Zones because they are so hard to identify. I was happy that they understood the potential challenges of the Yellow Zone, but I assured them that there was nothing to fear. Once you become aware, you have power.

Are you willing to acknowledge and nurture your Green Zones?

You might think that having Green Zones in your home guarantees an easy life. It's not that simple. Green Zones feel great to live in, but they also require a great deal of care and maintenance. If not attended to, Green Zones can shift to Yellow, or even Red, surprisingly quickly.

People who live in predominantly Green Zones typically:

- Accept responsibility for themselves and their emotions, and make feeling good their personal priority
- Embody self-love and self-respect
- Know how to align energy to what they want, consciously or unconsciously
- Acknowledge that they have choices in life
- Seek and welcome help
- Have a high awareness of their surroundings, feelings, and personal preferences
- Have a passion and a curiosity for life
- Live from love for themselves and others
- Are willing to do the work needed to have what they want, physically, emotionally, and spiritually
- Have faith in the Universe's ability to deliver what they want in perfect time

If you already love your home as it is right now, appreciate it, and remember that change is constant. Keeping your Green Zones green requires ongoing Awareness and care.

Green Zone challenges

- Green Zones carry a risk of sliding into complacency over time and not noticing when the feel of the space changes.
- When you love your home, you can sometimes experience fear of losing what you have.

Do what works for you

The key to learning about yourself and how you are through your home is to know that no matter what you are calling Red, Green, or Yellow right now, your perceptions of yourself and your home will change as you raise your personal vibration. If it is easier for you, you can forget about identifying colors or zones. Just go for feeling better and you will be fine, no matter where you are right now.

Take action that feels good and brings results. Do what works for you. Be prepared to ask yourself:

What are you willing to let go of?

What are you willing to let in?

Summary of Willingness

- Willingness goes beyond the physical work of creating Receiving Condition; Willingness includes letting go of resistant thoughts, feelings, and beliefs.
- You and your home are energetically intertwined. Change is easier when you shift the vibration of one and then the other, step-by-step.
- Raising your vibration is easier when you are able to recognize the underlying emotions at home, especially in your Red and Yellow Zones. As you are able to acknowledge and shift resistant thoughts, feelings, and beliefs, you will be pulled into action.
- Red Zones can feel overwhelming at first, and are easiest to shift step-by-step. If you have a lot of Red Zones, gently remind yourself that your home does not reflect who you are, it reflects *how* you are, and you can change that.
- Yellow Zones can be difficult to identify because there is nothing obviously wrong with them, and that is fine. You will be able to identify Yellow Zones more easily over time as you expand your Awareness and Desire.
- As beautiful as Green Zones are to live in, they still require ongoing care and attention to detail in order to maintain their vibration.
- Greater Willingness comes in layers through greater Awareness and Desire.

Now that you are familiar with The 3 Keys, Awareness, Desire, and Willingness, you are ready to put them into daily practice.

Part Three:
The 3 Keys into Practice

Awareness, Desire & Willingness into Practice

It doesn't matter what you know. It matters what you *do* with what you know.

By now, you should have the following:

- Basic understanding that your home works like a traffic light to The Universe, either resisting or welcoming what you want to have and experience in life
- A good idea of the color zones (energy zones) in your home to use as your starting point: Red, Yellow, and Green
- A written list of clear Desires, both general and specific, based on how you want your home to look and feel, along with a Personal Statement of Home
- A new level of Awareness to help you recognize limiting beliefs you hold about your home and yourself
- A new level of Willingness to look at your limiting thoughts and beliefs and let them go

You might feel some relief already, even if nothing around you has changed, yet. The feel of your home will shift as you allow yourself to think more encouraging thoughts.

Let's look now at how you can:

- Raise the vibration of your Red Zones to Yellow
- Raise the vibration of your Yellow Zones to Green
- Maintain, strengthen, and expand your Green Zones

Even if you are eager to get started, read through this next section on how to shift the energy in your home *before* you get into action, or at least while you are in action if you have already started. There are some very important principles and guidelines to help you get good results and keep you from getting your energy "zapped."

Chapter Six
Shifting a Red Zone

When you work on a Red Zone, the goal is to shift the energy to Yellow. The shift from Red to Yellow is huge, and is where you start. More receptive Green energy will come over time.

If you are eager to live in a Green vibration, keep in mind that your own personal energy needs to shift to match your living space so that you can sustain any changes you make. Even if you think you are ready for a big shift, go gently. If you take dramatic physical action to change your Red Zones and are not a match to the changes, your thoughts and emotions will continue to create resistance, and your home will slide back into a Red Zone. Make adjustments that you can sustain and that encourage you to keep moving forward. If you take on too much, too quickly, you will get overwhelmed, especially when shifting a Red Zone.

Remember—baby steps.

Decide where to start

Where would you most like to make a shift? Look at the floor plan you did when you identified the vibrational zones in your home. It is best to start with a small project and work your way up to the bigger ones.

Scan your home in your mind and choose the starting place that feels most exciting to you. Typically, the three most important rooms are your kitchen, bedroom, and bathroom. These are the primary rooms in which self-nurturing takes place. You decide.

Once you have chosen where you want to start, picture what you want there. Feel it. Get excited. Remember, if you're thinking about it, the Universe responds, so think of how you want that space to feel. Think, too, of how *you* want to feel.

Make an action plan

An action plan, even a basic one, helps keep you from feeling overwhelmed. Assemble tools to help you complete what you start.

For example, if your project is to clean out a kitchen drawer, you might want a garbage bin, a recycle bin, and a charity box, along with a damp towel for cleaning. Have these items ready to go. You might want a pen and paper to make notes for any ideas that come to you as you work.

If you are tackling your bedroom closet, assemble bags or boxes to bundle things up for charity.

Decide how much time you are going to spend—not too much and not too little. Just as with physical exercise, you want to push yourself enough for a good stretch and to build muscle, but not so much that you overstress. Thirty minutes to an hour often takes you to your mental and emotional saturation point when working in a Red Zone, especially at the beginning. See how you do and adjust accordingly.

Know your power is right here, right now

If you feel overwhelmed just thinking about the tasks before you, take heart. What you do now is far more powerful than anything you have done or thought in the past. You, your life, and your home are a reflection of your past thoughts, feelings, and actions. You have the power to create anything you want from this moment forward.

If you feel overwhelmed, think of this old joke:

Q. How do you eat an elephant?

A. One bite at a time.

The Golden Rule of Action: Take action only from a place of feeling good

I like to say that I have no rules, only guidelines and principles, but here is one important rule: Take action only from a place of feeling good.

If action comes purely from force or determined self-discipline, it will not be sustainable. You will be better off if you take action for only 5 minutes while feeling excited or hopeful or even neutral rather than force yourself into action for an hour while feeling overwhelmed, resentful, angry, or frustrated. It is possible to be so determined to get into action that you sabotage yourself. Remember, Willingness is more than determination. Willingness includes learning to dissolve emotional resistance and becoming receptive to change.

If you notice you are feeling reluctant, resentful, regretful, overwhelmed, helpless, angry, or anything strongly negative or resistant, do not take action. Action taken from a place of negative emotion simply cannot bring good results. If you try to work from a place of resistant emotion, you will not get far.

A little bit of resistance is natural and perfectly fine, but if the thought of taking action really doesn't feel good, do something else. Go for a walk. Take a nap. Write out your feelings to release your emotions. Sit outside and breathe in fresh air. Do something to help you feel stronger. Think about what would be helpful to you. Think of what you want. Picture your home transformed and feel relief.

Work on feeling good before all else. Then take action.

Consistency

Once you get into the habit of moving yourself into a good-feeling frame of mind, you will find that you are taking action all the time. Consistent action is the key to shifting the energy of your home. Without ongoing action, your home will slip back into disorder. As you shift your thoughts, you will find yourself in action without even trying.

You will find the right action at the right time—and sometimes *any* action is the right action!

If you can't figure out where to start, start anywhere! Just get yourself feeling good—and start!

Before you begin, shield yourself

When you are dealing with the energy of a Red Zone, the effects on your physical body can go far beyond what you would expect for the physical exertion involved. I once asked a large group of professional organizers if they ever experienced headaches, backaches, or unexplained moodiness after working in clients' homes, and a sea of hands flew up to say they did. That's because they were affected by the energy in the space. Learn to shield yourself from that energy before you begin.

- Make sure you are grounded and connected (see Exercise for grounding and connecting, Chapter 3). Breathe.
- Imagine a protective bubble of powerful white energy all around you.
- Set your unconscious Awareness to notice right away if your energy is getting zapped.
- Drink water.

In addition to being physically demanding, shifting a Red Zone can trigger underlying emotions such as frustration, anger, sadness, guilt, and grief. Go easy. Action by itself is not enough to shift a Red Zone. Often there is a need to release old beliefs or emotional hurt. Be willing to acknowledge whatever unpleasant emotion is there and let it go. If you don't know what emotion is there, that's fine. Acknowledge that there is something there and ask the Universe to help you to let it go. Say thank you in advance for the emotional release. Don't worry about doing this right—just have the genuine intention and willingness to release and you will feel the difference.

Monitor your thoughts and emotions

As you begin to take action in your Red Zone, it is normal to have resistant thoughts and emotions. Notice them. Remember, Awareness is your point of power.

Even if you are trying really hard to be in action, resistant emotions (guilt, anger, sadness, frustration, overwhelm) can keep you stuck, or at least slow you down.

For example, as you begin to work in a Red Zone, you may have thoughts like these:

- *Why is this up to me? I don't want to do this.*
- *I have no idea how to deal with this. I can't do it.*
- *I hate this. I hate this. I hate this.*
- *How did I let this happen?*

- *When will this ever end?*

That's okay. Let those thoughts roll out. And then change them:

- *Why is this up to me? I don't want to do this, but it is up to me because I am choosing to change my life. And if that means I have to suck it up and take this on, then I can handle it. It will be worth it to feel the relief.*
- *I have no idea how to deal with this. I can't do it. Yes, I can. I may not know what to do just yet, but I will figure it out, because I am not living like this anymore. I am changing my life one step at a time. I am not the same person who created this mess, and the person I am now can deal with it.*
- *I hate this. I hate this. I hate this. But then, I never want to do much, which is how I got into this mess. It will be easier once I get started.*
- *How did I let this happen? It doesn't matter how I got here. What matters is that I am dealing with it now, and I am changing things for good.*
- *When will this ever end? Well, there's only one way to find out, and I am going to do it.*

Do you see what happens when you catch yourself going into negative thoughts and make the conscious effort to change them? When your Awareness is accompanied by *receptive* emotions (hopefulness, eagerness, optimism, acceptance, forgiveness), it becomes easier to move into expanded Desire and Willingness—and action. Receptive thoughts and emotions are the key to moving forward.

Every once in a while, you may need to have a big rant. Go for it. Do it alone, and let it all out. Speak your frustrations, your anger, your hurt, out loud—whatever is there. Rant, scream, even stomp your feet or jump up and down if you feel like it. When you have let it all out, feel the relief flow through your body and then carry on.

When you feel yourself being discouraged by what you have to deal with, change your focus and get inspired by what is possible. Notice your feelings. If you experience negative emotion, there is something you can learn about yourself and heal.

Take action, even a tiny bit. Monitor yourself, take breaks, and get help if you need it. Make sure you have water and healthy snacks. A Red Zone and low blood sugar are not a good combination! Encourage yourself and allow yourself to feel relief and gratitude as you clear things out.

Note: You might find that playing upbeat music helps you to maintain momentum in this process. Experiment. Sometimes you might find that you prefer to work in quiet. Notice which feels better, and know that it can change from day to day, depending on what you are doing.

How resistance can help you

When you notice you are still feeling resistant to letting go of things in your home, even when you "know" The 3 Keys, see if you can find the underlying belief or vibration that is triggering the resistance.

For example, if you are hanging on to your grandmother's dining room set that you never really liked, or your father's collection of aviation books that you have never looked at, or your mother's wedding china that you never use, ask yourself what you are saying or "vibrating" out to the Universe by keeping it.

Why we hang on to things we don't really want

Here are some underlying beliefs or vibrations for hanging on to things you do not truly want:
- *I carry my past with me. I have no choice.*
- *I accept the burden of other people's stuff. It's my duty to keep things.*
- *I have a responsibility to honor my family.*

Notice what happens when you change those statements to:
- *What is most important to me is the now, the present. I release my past.*
- *I am free to decide what I keep in my life. I choose.*
- *I honor my family in who I am and what I do, not in what I keep.*

If you try to let things go and are still unable to release the things that do not serve you, you are not yet at the stage of true Willingness. That's okay. Just recognize it and explore what is holding you back. You will get there.

Exercise for releasing items you don't use

Think of three items that you have been holding on to but do not use. Some considerations are furniture, dishes, clothing, memorabilia, exercise equipment, books, and magazines, but it could be anything.

1. _____
2. _____
3. _____

For each item, write down what self-limiting statement you are making to the Universe by hanging on to it.

1. _____
2. _____
3. _____

Now, for each item, write a self-empowering statement to release you.

1. _____
2. _____
3. _____

You will know if you are getting to the root issue if your release statement gives you a feeling of relief and a new Willingness to take action.

Review the underlying vibrations of a Red Zone (See Chapter 3.)

Ask yourself if that is the energy you want to live in. When you get your answer, go back and review the Desires you wrote down. As you look at your Desires, get into feeling as if you already have what you want, and say thank you. This is a good time to make sure that you are grounded and connected, too.

Once you have spent a few minutes steeped in your Desires, check again to see how it feels to let go of things that no longer serve you.

Do you notice a difference? Affirm: *"I clear the path for good things to come to me. I release all that no longer serves me."*

Note: If you do *not* experience resistant emotions when shifting your Red Zones, more than likely you already shifted your personal energy before you started, which makes the physical work much easier.

Inherited items: good or bad?

Inherited items can be wonderful, so don't cart the family china out to the curb just yet! You may have a number of inherited items that you love, treasure, and use. Keep them and enjoy them.

It is when you hold on to inherited items by default, out of a sense of obligation or even simply through inertia that keeping them is not in your best interest. If keeping your grandmother's wing chair stops you from buying a chair that is more your taste or style, you are better off to let it go. But if you genuinely love the chair and enjoy sitting in it, keep it. If the fabric is worn or not to your taste, consider having the chair re-upholstered, but keep it.

Keeping inherited items purely out of sentimentality or a sense of obligation, especially if they take up much room, can get in the way of experiencing Receiving Condition in your home.

Does family stuff have a hold on you? Let it go!

I inherited my grandmother's bedroom suite when I was in my early twenties. For ten years, I moved that bedroom furniture with me, to three different cities. Twice I put it into paid storage at great expense. When I moved in with my husband, he told me he didn't like the bedroom set and didn't want to keep it. At first, I was surprised, but then I suddenly realized that I didn't like the furniture either, and never had. It was good quality and in good condition but ornate and old-fashioned, and it had only a double mattress. I had never considered whether I liked it or not. It was my grandmother's, so I kept it. Once I had perspective, I put the bedroom set up for auction, got a good price for it, and said, "Thank you, Grandma." And my husband and I got a new queen-size bed!

What inherited items do you have that are not your style?

Cutting the ties of family obligations

When I decided I no longer wanted a lovely antique drop leaf table that belonged to my great-aunt, I called a cousin who said she would love to have it. Although I would have given her the table happily, I decided to offer it to her for a small price instead. I realized that if I gave her the table, she would receive it as a family heirloom and a gift, potentially creating a sense of obligation. Because I sold it to her, it is hers to use, sell, give away, or whatever she wants, with no obligation to me or to our great-aunt.

Remember your family through stories, not stuff.

My sister's three young children came to our house for a sleepover one night and forgot to bring their storybooks. At bedtime, I improvised by telling them stories from my childhood. I come from a large family, so we had many funny tales from Christmas and birthdays, stories about my parents and grandparents, some of which I had heard from my parents. We rolled around laughing. My sister's kids never brought another book to our house. We made a tradition of family storytelling that carries on to this day. Now they are young adults and have a much greater sense of family through the stories they now know by heart than from any amount of heirloom furniture.

Affirmations

Affirmations are statements that help you feel better (i.e. more receptive). Using affirmations can be powerful in helping you shift your vibration. Choose affirmations that feel good to you, those that evoke feelings of relief or hope or possibility. Use them to help you feel good before and while doing the physical work in your living space.

Sample affirmations for clearing a Red Zone:

I am creating my new life experience, now. My past is past.
I welcome new energy into my life. I release the old.
I invite love and beauty into my life. I am worthy.
I let go of chaos.
I am in charge of my home and my life.
It is safe for me to move forward.
I release all that is keeping me in the past. I am free.
I am ready for ease.
I make room for newness in my life.
I choose.

Especially when you are working through Red Zones, affirmations can be more powerful when you acknowledge what is there for you emotionally right now. Walking around chanting, "I'm so happy, I'm so happy, I'm so happy," when deep inside you feel sad or scared or angry, isn't helpful. Affirmations must feel real in order to work. If you are feeling resistance, try starting your affirmation with "Even though..."

Even though I feel scared/angry/sad, I am ready to move forward with ease.

Even though I hate this with every cell in my body, I know I can get through it.

Even though this feels exhausting already, I can manage if I take it step by step.

Even though I am nervous and worried about what is here, it feels good to start.

Even though I feel totally overwhelmed, I have the help and support I need to get me through this.

Now, practice writing some affirmations of your own, using whatever language works for you:

Even though _____

_____

Even though _____

_____

Even though _____

_____

Even though _____

_____

Even though _____

_____

Play with word variations until you find the affirmations that feel right for you. Everyone has personal responses to different words or phrases.

> *"All healing is release from the past."*
> *—A Course in Miracles*

Keep it manageable

Completion is the key to making progress in a Red Zone. If you try to take on an entire room in a day and get it only partway done, you will feel discouraged. But if you take on just one drawer, one cupboard, or one tabletop and get it cleaned and organized, you will have a sense of accomplishment.

If you feel up for more when you finish one thing, you can take on another chunk. As much as you will be eager to get things done, it will be easier if you take things one step at a time. Taking just one piece of clothing out of an overstuffed closet each day might not seem like a lot, but if you stayed with it over time, you would see progress (365 days in a year = 365 items gone!).

Work at a level that you can sustain. Push yourself a little more as you start to feel good with your results. But start.

Tackle one shelf in your linen closet, one drawer in your kitchen, one corner of your kitchen counter, the floor of your entrance hall, your bathroom counter, your bedside table, one bookshelf, your coffee table, your dining room table, or one corner of your living room. Do something every day.

Continue to be aware of how things in your home translate into energetic messages to the Universe.

If you haven't cleaned your refrigerator for six months or a year, what are you saying? Here are some possible underlying vibrations:

- *The details of my life are not important to me.*
- *I allow things to go stale and rotten in my life.*

Notice what happens when you change these messages to:

- *Everything in my life is fresh, clean, and healthy. I delight in the details of my life.*

Do you see how this works?

The key is to shift your point of vibration. Everything is energy! All of your action will flow from how you feel.

The magic of twenty minutes

A client whose house was a total Red Zone by anyone's estimation told me that the best advice I gave her was to do twenty minutes of clearing in her bedroom every night. Twenty minutes of focused, determined, enthusiastic purging and organizing. No more, no less. After twenty minutes, she could relax, watch television, do whatever she wanted. The next time I stopped by the house, I could not believe the difference in her room—and in her. She was so pleased with herself and her progress that she was determined to keep going. She still had a lot of work to do, but she no longer felt overwhelmed.

Begin with 20 minutes a day. Even 5 minutes. Just start.

Don't be a martyr or a hero—get help

We live in a do-it-yourself culture, which is not always healthy. Learn to ask for help, especially when you feel stuck. Enlisting help, paid or unpaid, is a great way to commit and have someone to help you stay focused. If you have friends or family you can ask to help you, great. Plan a specific task and a timeframe. Remember, even with help, you might reach your limit faster than you think in a Red Zone. Don't be surprised if you feel tired after just thirty minutes or an hour. Monitor how you are doing and keep an eye on your helpers, too. Clearing a Red Zone is not always fun.

Sometimes it is easier to have a helper who has no personal connection with you. You do not have to be wealthy to have paid help. There are many good workers willing to work for surprisingly little money, so ask around.

Even professional organizers are often affordable, and worth the money. If paying someone is out of the question, get creative. Trade a few hours of work with a friend or sell a few items and use the money to hire help. Once you decide to make the shift and feel truly ready to do it, you will come up with lots of ideas! Just decide.

Note: No amount of extra help, paid or unpaid, is going to help you unless you are willing to make changes. I have spoken to many professional organizers who say that one of their biggest frustrations is not being able to help clients who say they want to clear things out but are simply not emotionally ready to let things go. Asking for help is great, but you have to be ready.

Dramatic action can work, too

Taking baby steps is important, especially at the beginning, but you may get to the stage where you are ready for more dramatic action. If you have been doing your personal work, if you have been changing your thoughts, noticing and releasing resistant emotions, spending a few minutes every day in heartfelt gratitude, and strengthening your Desires, you may be ready to take a bigger step forward. If you can look at your living space and feel chills of excitement at the thought of how it will be instead of dread at how it is, you are ready to graduate from baby steps to big steps. Hire a couple of helpers for a full day, book a truck to pick up a load for charity, have a monster garage sale, or even do all three. You will be able to come up with literally hundreds of ideas for action when you are ready.

Commit to a deadline

Pick a project and give yourself a deadline to finish it. Set yourself up for success. Make a short but workable deadline. If you put your deadline too far out in the future, it won't have any pull. If there are things that you want to clear out of your house, book a charity pick-up for a specific day. If you don't have a charity that offers pick up in your area, mark a day on the calendar to take a carload to a charity drop-off depot. If you don't have a car, make a date with a friend to drive you. If you don't have a friend with a car, take a taxi. Do whatever it takes—no excuses. Make a commitment and follow through.

Notice how you feel

As you clear things out, you will start to notice how much better your home feels. Your space will feel lighter, and so will you.

Wondering does wonders!

You don't need to be an expert organizer, designer, or handyperson to have a home that supports you in living a life that you love. A powerful way to spark ideas is to wonder. Instead of "But I don't know how to…" or "But I don't have the money to…" try "I wonder how I could…" and notice the difference.

Start to wonder:

I wonder what it would take to…
I wonder if I could find someone to help me…
I wonder if there is a way to…
I wonder if there is an easier way to…
I wonder how I could…
I wonder if there is a…
I wonder what would look good….
I wonder if there might be a different way to…
I wonder how much it would cost to…

If you need a how-to on anything, great resources are available on anything related to organizing or decorating your home. Don't let yourself get bogged down in décor details, especially in a Red Zone. Go ahead and picture how you want things to be, but work on getting things cleared out, clean, and organized. Stay focused on what you are trying to achieve, and things will be much easier.

Clean and tidy before all else

The number-one prerequisite for living in Receiving Condition is having a clean and tidy home. If your house is not clean and tidy, it is not in Receiving Condition. Period.

Is mess always bad?

Short-lived mess from time to time, and from room to room, can be fine and natural, even healthy sometimes, if you are aware of it. There are times when life gets busy and you give yourself permission to let things go for a little bit. It's okay for your house to have an occasional "pajama day," or even two. But if that pajama day turns into a pajama week or a pajama month, it will start to clog up the energy in your home. Mess needs to be tidied and cleaned before long or it will weigh you down. Old mess feels heavier than new mess. Start to notice. If you need a guideline for how long mess can hang around before it becomes an energetic weight on you, think in hours rather than days.

If you have learned to live with dirt and disorder in your home and still feel reasonably happy, you have an opportunity to be nicer to yourself. No matter what you consider to be normal or tolerable, there is *never* a time when living in a dirty, messy home is in your best interest. Ongoing mess leads to a dirty mess, and whether you are conscious of it or not, dirt and mess bog you down. Clean and tidy will always serve you best.

You can feel clean before you see it

I am not a clean freak, really. In fact, I have spent most of my life being very messy. Years ago, when I was still single, I invited a group of people back to my apartment after a conference dinner. As I had the key in my door, I warned my guests that my place was going to look like someone had broken in. And it did. That was just the way I lived—in chaos. But at the time, I was a mess inside, too, and it showed in how my apartment looked. As I have done my personal healing, I have become cleaner and neater without even trying. Now I can't tolerate dirt and mess because I notice that it doesn't feel good. It no longer matches me and my vibration.

One of my biggest surprises about working in people's houses has been how much dirt there can be in homes that at first glance look clean. As you become more aware of energy, you will come to notice a heavy, stagnant feel in a dirty house. Whether in your own home or someone else's, you will be able to *feel* whether a house is clean or dirty without needing to look.

Clean requires movement

Receiving Condition requires motion, and that includes moving things when you clean. We once discovered two years' worth of dust and dirt under the loveseat of a client whose condo was professionally cleaned regularly. Apparently, the cleaner didn't move furniture. I have seen years of accumulated dust behind beds, in closets, and behind dressers in what appeared at first to be relatively clean houses. I don't want to tell you what we have seen behind stoves and refrigerators.

As you clean, notice how much lighter everything feels.

Go easy on yourself. There is no need to stress or obsess. You will find as I did that your need for clean and tidy will rise with your general feeling of well-being.

A good vacuum cleaner is a must

Cleaning properly requires time and attention to detail—and a good vacuum cleaner. This might seem obvious, but it's not. We had lovely, smart clients who chose not to own a vacuum cleaner because they had no carpeting and thought they could clean well enough with a broom and a mop. They were mistaken. The professional cleaners who came in filled an entire vacuum bag when they cleaned, something they said had never happened before. Clean requires regular vacuuming.

You don't have to be the one who cleans

It takes a lot of work to keep any house clean, especially if you have a busy life. If you do not already have a cleaning person, get one. Keeping a house clean and tidy, even when you have someone to come in and do the big jobs, takes time. If you're thinking, *"Right, I'm going to have someone else come in and clean my house, like that's going to happen!"* think again. Anyone can have help; it's not a privilege reserved for the well-to-do. All you have to do is decide. The person who repaired the bricks on our house has someone clean his apartment every week. He told me he would much rather work a few extra hours doing what he is good at in order to pay for someone else to clean for him. He's not wealthy, but I wouldn't be surprised if, one day soon, he will be, because he is smart about where he spends his time and energy. Do whatever is necessary to get some help. Choose cleaning services over a new pair of shoes, dinner out, or a new phone. Be resourceful. You can do it if you choose. You decide.

If you can't find a cleaning person right away, or truly don't have the money right now, barter with a friend to help you—it makes the job easier and faster. If you can't afford help every week or every other week in the beginning, get someone to clean once a month, once a season or even once a year. Just get some help!

Make sure that whoever comes into your home is competent and trustworthy. We have had well-meaning cleaning people do costly damage in our home just because they didn't know any better. If at all possible, be at home when your cleaners come the first time. And make sure that the person you hire enjoys cleaning, because you want happy energy in your home.

Don't presume that just anyone can clean well. Good, professional cleaning is a real skill that is undervalued and under-respected in our culture.

More tips and guidelines for shifting your Red Zones

Clutter

Most people hold on to things that they wouldn't notice missing if they disappeared. That's why storage facilities hold regular auctions of the contents of units in default of payment. I've often said that if I could invent one thing, it would be a *disappear-er*, a wand you could just point at things to make them disappear so you didn't have to decide what to do with them. Since we don't have that invention yet, there's still a little more work to it.

The physical clearing of clutter is the easy part. You can hire people to do that for you. It's the emotional component that will trip you up.

Clutter has emotional roots. If you have been trying to get rid of clutter without success, it is because you are still an energetic match with it. Until you can change the thoughts, feelings, and beliefs that are creating the clutter, even if you clear things out, more will appear. But as you release your resistant thoughts, it becomes easier to clear out clutter—for good. If you are going in circles, get your thoughts and feelings going in a straight, happy, hopeful line forward, and notice the difference.

Take care to get "purged" items out of your house immediately. Don't risk changing your mind and letting those boxes and bags become more clutter! If you have worked from a place of feeling good, you will be able to trust your decisions and let things go with peace of mind.

Note: Make an effort to choose eco-friendly methods for disposing of your purged items. Check your local guidelines and resources for disposal and recycling.

Cash out your clutter

There are many avenues by which you can get money for your stuff, especially now, with the Internet.

A traditional yard sale is still a great way to clear things out, depending on what you have to sell and where you live. The purpose of a yard sale, apart from generating a bit of cash, is to get rid of things, so whatever goes out, stays out. My husband and I had a garage sale several years ago that had enough in it to cover a four-car driveway. Pretty much everything in the sale was mine. Back then I didn't know anything about getting rid of stuff. I just moved everything I owned around with me, at great expense. By noon of the yard sale, we were giving things away just to be done with it. Later that day, I told my husband that I couldn't name three things we had sold that morning; they were already gone from my memory! It felt very freeing.

There is endless how-to information on line about how to organize a yard sale or sell things in any number of ways, if you need it. Many websites are out there to help you find buyers for your things. Please use good sense when dealing with unknown buyers. Do not meet with a stranger alone, and do not accept a personal check for payment. Exercise good judgment.

> **Are you looking for someone "worthy" of your stuff? Stop, and let it go!**
>
> *I put my grandmother's old color television on our front lawn with a sign that said "Free." The television still worked well and had a good picture and a remote control, but because of its age had a limited range of channels. It might seem funny to be sentimental about a television set, but that one held a lot of wonderful memories for me. When I saw someone stop to look at it, I caught myself watching, trying to see if the person looked "worthy" of my grandmother's television. When I realized what I was doing, I gave myself a shake and let it go.*

Books

I have seen people weighed down with boxes upon boxes of books that have not been unpacked for years, and walls of shelves spilling over with books. If you love books and have a lot of them, do yourself a favor and start to see your books in a new light. Keeping books is not a bad thing. In fact, having books around can be good energy if you have books you love and arrange them carefully and logically on shelves that are integrated beautifully into your living space.

Books are meant to uplift you, not weigh you down. Be selective. Keep the books that you love, that you need for reference, that support your interests, and that are consistent with what you want to bring more of into your life, and let the rest go. If you have cookbooks that you haven't made a recipe from in over a decade, let them go. If you have novels you read three summers ago, let someone else enjoy them now. If you have a twenty-year-old copy of Moby Dick that you still haven't read, unburden yourself. And if you still have your Grade 10 Geography textbook, I hope that's an easy call. Release the books that no longer serve you and treat the ones you keep with care and respect.

One client was holding on to accounting books from a course she had taken over twenty years before. When I asked her about them, she told me that she regretted not having finished her studies and thought that keeping the books would give her hope that she would one day go back to school. The problem was that the books did not give her hope; every time she looked at them, she felt regret and disappointment. The books reinforced a feeling of failure. When she saw that, she was able to let them go, and the feeling of failure along with them. What books do you have that you would be better off without?

You can sell your books, give them to friends, give them to charities or your local library, or put them in a box in front of your house, offering them free to anyone who wants to take and enjoy. And more often than you might believe, some books belong in the recycle bin.

The energy of books

One time when I spoke at a conference, a man asked me if his collection of books about war carried a negative vibration. I suggested that having books about war wasn't necessarily a bad thing, if the study of war was driven by a love of history and a desire for peace. I asked him why he had the books and how he felt about them. I could tell from talking to him that he was far more interested in peace than war. When he realized that the books made him feel good, he was greatly relieved.

What about your children's storybooks?

Children's books can spark complex emotions. Be willing to look at why you are keeping things so you can make an informed choice.

For example, if you are keeping shelves or boxes filled with your now grown children's childhood storybooks, you might be thinking that it would be nice for your grandchildren to read those same books, like a family tradition. That sounds reasonable, right? Yet, consider the possible underlying message. Test out these statements to see if one might apply:

- *These books help me remember when my children were little. They were so cute, and it has all gone by so quickly (sigh).*
- *These books show what a good job I did of parenting, and I want to keep them as evidence.*
- *My children will need these books for their children. I want to be needed.*
- *I am concerned that my children won't choose good books for their kids.*
- *I want to manage how my children parent their children. I need to make sure they do a good job.*

Or perhaps you are simply thinking that they are good, expensive books, so why not keep them. That sounds reasonable and practical, right? Yet, look at some possible underlying messages this thought might be reflecting:

- *I am worried that my children won't be able to afford to buy books for their children. I'm not sure I have confidence in my children's ability to provide for their children.*
- *I am scared I won't have money to buy things for my grandchildren. At least if I keep these books, I know I will have something to give them.*

If you have been holding on to your children's books for years after they finished with them, consider this:

- The books are unavailable for other children to enjoy.
- Your children may live far away by the time they have children, and the books may never be used or enjoyed again.
- Your children may prefer to choose books for their own children.
- There may be even better children's books available to your grandchildren by the time they are ready for them.
- Your grandchildren might like completely different books from those your children enjoyed.
- Unless you are keeping the books safely in archival conditions, they are at risk of becoming musty or moldy and of no value to anyone.

There is nothing inherently wrong with keeping your children's books. Go ahead and keep them if it is important to you. Just be willing to look at *why* you are keeping them. Maybe you will decide to keep your favorites, ask your children to choose their favorites, and give the rest away so that other children can benefit, now. If you wanted to, you could start a book savings fund now so that you can buy books for your grandchildren later according to their personalities and interests.

As with anything, release when you are ready.

Move your but!

The words you use and how you use them directly affect the energy you give out. One little three-letter word can change everything. Listen to what happens when you use the word *but* after a statement of what you want:

I want a new _____ but it's way too expensive.

I'd love to _____ but I don't know how I would be able to do it.

I would love a _____ but I don't think that's ever going to happen.

What I would really like is a _____ but we just don't have the room.

But, but, but, but, but, but…! Do you see how you sabotage yourself by using the word *but* after stating what you want?

Now, move your but and feel the difference!

Notice how different these statements feel when you move your *but:*
I would love a new kitchen, **but** *we just don't have the money.* (powerless)
We don't have the money, **but** *I would love a new kitchen.* (possible)

I am ready to clear things out, **but** *my husband is a packrat.* (powerless)
My husband is a packrat, **but** *I am ready to clear things out.* (possible)

I would love to move, **but** *we can't really afford it right now.* (powerless)
We can't really afford it right now, **but** *I would love to move.* (possible)

I would love a new couch, **but** *I hate shopping for furniture.* (powerless)
I hate shopping for furniture, **but** *I would love a new couch.* (possible)

Can you notice the difference that moving the word *but* makes? Doing something as simple as moving one word changes the vibration of your words from *powerless* to *possible*. When you hear yourself sabotaging you with *but*, whether aloud or in your thoughts, catch yourself and move the statement around so that it feels better.

Saving your stuff for the future?

There may be things that you want to save for the future, but let's face it, you will never use most of the things you save. Look around you and see what you are holding on to that you would be better off releasing.

My sister called me one day to share her excitement at cleaning out her kitchen cupboards. She had taken an old set of dishes out of the cupboard and put them in the basement to keep for her then teenage daughter's first apartment. I encouraged her to give the dishes away and let her daughter choose her own when the time came, but she decided to keep them. Later that day, she found out that a family in her neighborhood had just lost everything in a house fire. The family had received clothing and bedding from the community, but no dishes. My sister was thrilled to give the old dishes to the family in need, and when the time came, my niece got lovely new dishes for her first apartment.

What are you keeping for the future that someone else could use right now?

Keep only what you really want and use, and let the rest go

My parents moved from southern Ontario to the coast of New Brunswick just after my father's eightieth birthday. They had been spending summers in St. Andrews for many years and decided it was time to live full-time in one place.

Despite having previously downsized from their rambling six-bedroom home of forty years to a two-bedroom townhome, somehow they had managed to hold on to a surprising amount of stuff. In fact, just before they moved east, they bought a second three-bedroom home that my father called the most expensive storage unit in the world. When my parents were in New Brunswick, waiting for the moving truck to arrive from Ontario, my mother told me that she kept hoping to get a phone call telling her that the truck had gone over a cliff. For me, my mother's confession said it all. People spend so much time and energy—and money!—hanging on to stuff that, deep down, they wish would disappear.

Not many years after that move, my parents died within fifteen months of each other. My sister and I were co-executors and went through Mom's and Dad's things to get their two properties ready to sell. Despite both homes appearing neat, clean, and uncluttered, we discovered boxes upon boxes of papers and letters. We found closets, drawers and cupboards filled to overflowing, plus a basement and a garage with still more.

At first, my sister and I were sad and weepy as we worked our way through my parents' things. After several exhausting eighteen-hour days, my sentimental side caved in when I found my parents' wedding certificate stuffed in a random box, next to a receipt for an oil change from 1964. Half-laughing, half-crying, I screamed out loud, "If you weren't dead, I'd kill you!" My sister and I allowed ourselves a short rant of "Just who did they think was going to go through all this and clean it up?" and then we returned to our duties with renewed strength and love. We made it through. Lots went to the dump, lots when to charity, some went to family friends, some furniture was left with the property, and everything else was shipped across the country, divided among the eight children.

What stuck with me the most was realizing the stress it had put on Mom and Dad to carry around all the stuff they had accumulated through the years, stuff that my mother had secretly hoped would fall off a cliff. It would have been so much easier for them (and for us) if they had purged and sorted along the way, and just let things go.

Repairs

Broken things hold negative energy. Leaky things leak energy. Broken things also cause low-level stress. It will serve you well to repair leaky faucets, broken handles, cracked windows, loose towel bars, doors that don't close, light fixtures—anything on your list, ideally as soon as it breaks. If you don't have a handyman or handywoman in the family, hire one, barter, ask around, and use your powers of attraction to find one! Be sure to get someone competent. The only thing more bothersome than something in disrepair is something repaired badly.

Two-minute miracles

Even if you have a regular cleaning service, the daily habit of short bursts of tidying and cleaning is essential to maintaining a home in Receiving Condition. If you are like me and do not like to clean house, doing a little bit all the time is the easiest way to manage. Ten seconds here, fifteen seconds there. Put a few things away, wipe a counter, close a cupboard door, re-position cushions. Don't obsess—just do. If you already have a clean and tidy home, you know that the job of keeping your living space in reasonable order never ends. It requires daily attention.

Here are a few ideas to get you started:

- Take thirty seconds to tidy the bathroom before you leave the house in the morning. Thirty seconds is enough time to pick up towels, put away toiletries, wipe the counters and sink, and put the toilet seat down.
- Take another thirty seconds to put dirty dishes in the dishwasher and wipe the kitchen counters after breakfast.
- Before you go to bed, take two minutes to tidy your bedroom. Put dirty clothes in the laundry basket, return clean clothes to the cupboard, and tidy up whatever is on your floor, dresser, or side table. Just two minutes can make a huge difference.

- Every day take thirty seconds to hang up coats and organize boots and shoes at the front door.
- Take two minutes to put in a load of laundry when you really don't feel like it.

Don't think about it too hard. Just do it. If it works for you, get a timer and see how much you can do in thirty seconds, one minute, or five minutes. Have some fun. You will find you begin to do this without even noticing. This habit of tidying up after yourself (and even a few other people, when necessary) is one of the best stress-busters around!

Here is my favorite under-four-minute miracle (I've timed it!): Unload the dishwasher as soon as the cycle is done. Nothing backs up a kitchen faster than having no place to put dirty dishes. If it's late at night and you want to go to bed, push yourself for just a few minutes. Come morning, you'll be glad you did.

Note: If you don't have a dishwasher, you might want to add one to your wish list!

Easy does it

When you are shifting a Red Zone, go easy on yourself. You are not going to reverse years of neglect and accumulation, and the emotions that go with them in a matter of hours, days, or even weeks. The goal is to feel good, so move at a pace that feels right. Remember, you are not fixing something; you are changing your life. Don't obsess; just be aware and active—every day.

Red Zones often carry heavy energy that can affect you physically and emotionally. One workshop participant told me that before she knew better, she had spent an entire weekend clearing out her basement. For three days afterwards, she felt inexplicably depressed, almost as if she was drugged, and she could not get out of bed. The heavy energy that was stirred up in her basement "zapped" her. Be careful that it does not happen to you. Take baby steps and monitor how you feel.

Note: After you have worked in a Red Zone, take a warm bath or shower and put your clothes directly into the laundry. It is important to clear your energy before going to bed or going on with the rest of your day.

All in good time

You may be able to take action right away on some tasks in your home, but other tasks may take more time. My husband and I have had things linger in disrepair, and sometimes I decide just to roll with it.

A few years ago, our shower developed a leak at a time when I knew my husband was not up to dealing with the demolition required to fix it. We had a nice, deep, separate bathtub with hand-held sprayer, and we had another shower in the basement for guests, so it made little difference to me that the shower was out of commission.

It took three years, but one day I came home and found piles of smashed shower tile outside our back door. My husband was suddenly ready to take action, and the shower was fixed in a short time. I was glad I hadn't pushed. It was so much easier on both of us, and no harm was done in the wait. In fact, it created a nice outcome. While we had no shower, my husband learned to love baths, which he still chooses over the shower most days!

Know when it is time to push and when it is time to allow things to unfold in their own time. The important part is getting yourself to feel good, excited, and hopeful, no matter where you are.

If you are still not in action, there is more healing to be done

If you have worked to raise your Awareness, Desire, and Willingness and have still not noticed a shift in how you feel, it may be that something within your home or within you needs to be cleared or healed, first. It does not mean that something is wrong with you; it just means that something is "stuck" and needs to be released. The stuck energy could be a deep limiting belief, a fear, or an old emotional wound. On the other hand, there could be some energy in your home that is affecting you. Whatever it is, with strong enough Awareness and Desire, you will have the Willingness to find the right help you need to shift the energy and move into action.

Note: There is a level of disorganization that is chronic and unhealthy. Chronic disorganization is living in an extreme mess and chaos for a long time with no indication of change, to the point where it affects your day-to-day living and becomes a concern to others. If you have a chronic issue, you will need to recognize it and choose to get help. Look online for local resources.

Chapter Seven
Shifting a Yellow Zone

Yellow Zones can be the trickiest areas to shift because they are the most difficult to identify. To notice and shift a Yellow Zone requires expanded Awareness along with expanded Desire. Only as you become aware of new options and want something new will you get the urge to shift your Yellow Zones and kick things up a notch. Otherwise, things will stay as they are.

It isn't necessarily bad when things stay the same, especially if your home is clean, tidy, and reasonably nice. However, keeping things the same for too long is not as likely to give you a home and a life that you *love*. Remember, Receiving Condition calls for motion.

What shifts a Yellow Zone to a Green Zone?

Once a Yellow Zone is reasonably clean and tidy, shifting it to a Green Zone is probably the most fun and exciting shift to make, because you are not dealing with as much "heavy energy" as exists in a Red Zone.

To shift the energy in your home, always go back to The 3 Keys, Awareness, Desire, and Willingness. If you have identified your Yellow Zone, you will already have a certain level of Awareness.

Now, work with your Desires. What look, feel and function do you want to create? What would make the space more welcoming, more functional, and more beautiful? Remember, wanting more doesn't mean that what you have is not good enough; it is simply part of the process of choosing to move forward. As you begin to wonder about what you might like, your thoughts will move naturally towards creating a Green Zone. If you are ready to make a shift, you will be curious, and feel excited thinking about new possibilities. When your Desire gets strong and specific enough, you will be drawn to a new level of Willingness and into action.

Exercise to shift a Yellow Zone

Think of a specific Yellow Zone in your home and reflect on your intention for the space. With each room or area, take a minute and imagine what you would like to create there.

- What is the most important function or feature of this space?
- How do you want it to look and feel?
- How do *you* want to feel when you are in this space?

Notice your emotional responses. You might still feel some resistance at first, and that is okay. The questions above and those that follow are intended to inspire you and help you see new possibilities; they are not intended to test or measure you. If you experience resistance, especially defensiveness, your emotional responses will tell you something about your readiness to make changes. If it feels like you need a nudge, forge ahead. If it feels more like you need a big push, you might need to give yourself more time.

> *"When you feel the need arise to be defensive about anything, you have identified yourself with an illusion."*
> —*A Course in Miracles*

Here are some considerations to help you generate ideas and inspiration. We will go through the various rooms in a house with an eye to how you can shift your home's Yellow vibration areas to Green. Write down ideas as they come to you.

Kitchen

Your kitchen is where you nourish yourself and your family. Look at your kitchen.

- Is this a kitchen that inspires healthy, happy living?
- Are your cupboards and drawers organized logically for optimum function? For example, are the cooking utensils near the stove and are the mixing bowls reasonably accessible to the baking supplies?
- Do you like and use everything in your drawers and cupboards?
- Do you have primarily healthy, nourishing food on hand?*
- What about your dishes? Do you like them? Are any pieces chipped or broken?
- Look at your towels. Are they fresh and new or worn and stained?
- Look at your kitchen utensils and cookware. What would be nice to replace or add?
- Are your kitchen counters clean and clear of all but a few things, such as your toaster and coffee maker?
- Does your décor need to be changed or updated: countertops, cupboards, paint colour, floors, light fixture?
- What about your appliances? Are they sparkling clean and in good working order? Is your refrigerator door clear of magnets and papers (feel the resistance….!)?
- Do you have enough lights, both overhead and under-cabinet?
- What about seating? Do you have comfortable, stylish stools or chairs?

Look at everything and make a note of what you would like to change.

Healthy Eating Tip: Your point of power is your point of purchase! I have found that if I buy potato chips, cookies, or ice cream, I eat them. If I don't buy them, I don't eat them. Simple, but it works!

Bedroom

Your bedroom is a place of rest and renewal and, if you choose, romance. Look at your bedroom.

- Is it a place of peace?
- Are the floors clear of clutter? Are they clean and beautiful?
- Are your closet and drawer contents pared down to only the clothes that you love and wear?
- Do you have a good quality mattress and luxurious bedding?
- Do you have nice art on the walls and pleasing wall color, along with good lighting, ideally on a dimmer switch?

- If you read in bed, do you have lamps with adjustable brightness that are placed at a good, functional height?
- Do your window coverings (blinds, curtains, shutters) allow you to control the amount of natural light easily from dark to light?
- Do you feel happy, relaxed and pampered in the space?
- Is the room free of electronics such as computer, television*, and anything that glows in the dark?

* **Note:** As a general rule, a television in your bedroom is not a healthy choice for either your sleep or your romantic relationships. However, you choose for yourself.

When my husband and I got together, I did not want a television in the bedroom, and he did not want our dog sleeping in bed with us. We compromised and ended up with both television and dog in the bedroom. After our dog died a few years ago, the television went out of the bedroom.

Last Christmas, after much soul-searching, I decided to give my husband a nice new television for our bedroom. He loves to watch television in bed as his way of relaxing, and I decided that it would give him so much pleasure that it was the right thing to do.

I was right. At least for now, it has been good for us. I do not encourage a television in the bedroom, and my husband has talked about taking it out again, but right now, it is what we choose. We are planning to redecorate our bedroom shortly, so we will see what happens.

Bathroom

Your bathroom is a place for your personal care. It is your first stop in the morning and your last stop at night. Look at your bathroom.

- Is it pristine? Is the counter space clean and clear?
- Are your personal care products good quality and as natural as possible, free of toxic ingredients and harmful perfumes?
- Do you have soothing décor? A beautiful candle?
- Do you have good quality, fresh-looking towels, shower curtain, and bath mat?
- Is there good, bright lighting on a dimmer switch?
- Are there enough shelves and cupboards to accommodate your bathroom products?

- Do you have a large, good quality mirror?
- How about a source of feel-good music?
- Is everything in good repair?
- What about your countertop, sink, and taps? Are they current in style and in good repair?
- What about your bathtub? Is it still gleaming or does it need to be replaced or refinished?
- What about bath tiles, flooring, towel bars, and other details, including your toilet brush?

Have a look and start to get excited about what you can change.

Note: For both hygienic and aesthetic reasons, toothbrushes need to be tucked away, out of sight, at all times. Find a clean, dry place to store toothbrushes in a drawer or cupboard.

Living room

Look at your living room.
- Does your living room invite reading and relaxation, good conversation, and activities with friends and family?
- Is there sufficient light? Is the light adjustable for reading and for ambiance?
- Is your furniture comfortable? Is it beautiful? Do you have nice cushions and a warm throw to snuggle up with? Does the furniture arrangement give you the best use of space?
- Do you have beautiful, original art on the walls?
- Is it a happy, welcoming, functional, comfortable, and useful space?
- Do you have or want to have a fireplace?
- Is there anything in your living room that you do not want, need, or use?
- Do you have current, functional window coverings?
- Are shelves beautiful, with books and decorative items carefully selected and arranged?
- Does anything look cluttered, from your new "going for Green" perspective?
- What about the flooring?
- Do you have a good sound system? Good music?
- Fresh flowers?

• What else would you like to add or change?

Look closely to see what's there. Expand your Desires as you feel inspired. Get excited about the possibilities.

Dining room

• Does your dining room feel warm and inviting?
• Do you use it to enjoy sit-down meals with friends and family?
• Is there sufficient light? Is the light fixture beautiful and in proportion to the space? Do you have a dimmer switch on the light to create ambiance?
• Is your dining table the right size and shape for your needs? Does it fit well in the space? Do you like how it looks?
• Are your chairs to your taste and comfortable?
• Is the space welcoming and attractive?
• What about your table linens, dishes, glassware and cutlery?
• Do you have art you love on the walls or maybe a mirror?
• Do the flooring and wall color work well? What about an area rug?

Notice what you have and what you like and make notes. If you would like to love and use your dining room more, what would it take?

Expanded appreciation counts in your energy

You may discover as you look around your home that you actually really like a lot more of what you already own than you realized. That's great. When you actively appreciate what you have and use it better, you contribute to a higher vibration in your home, even when technically nothing is new.

General considerations to boost a Yellow Zone to Green

Photos on display

It's fine to love your photos of family and friends, just check to see if they are taking over your home. Some people have so many photos on display that their home seems like a shrine. Use your intuition to decide how many photographs you want to have and where.

A concern I have about photos is that they are, by their nature, about the past. If you want your home to support you in living fully in the present and creating a future that you love, you probably don't want to overload it with images of the past. Honor your heritage and display pictures of people you love if that's important to you, but keep it in balance. Too much of the past in pictures can weigh you down and keep you from moving forward.

Notice your emotional responses to the photos you have around you. Photos of people who have died can help you feel their continued loving presence or they can spark a sense of sadness and loss. Photos of young children who are now grown can make you feel warm and happy or they can evoke a feeling of melancholy that time is passing by so quickly. Things in your home are meant to uplift you, so pay attention to what you have around you.

According to feng shui principles, if you are part of a couple, it is best to keep only pictures of yourselves as a couple in your bedroom so that the room remains your private space, without other people's eyes on you.

If you are single, it's generally not a good idea to display pictures of you alone, unless you want things to stay that way!

Children often like to have pictures of family in their rooms to help them feel connected and safe.

Once photos are framed, they seem to stay out on display forever. Don't be afraid to pack up framed pictures or change what's in the frame. Do it in a way that feels good and right to you. It's easy to keep all the photos you like in an album, or even just in a box, and look at them when you get the urge.

Being thoughtful and selective about which photos you keep on display will help you to make room for more beautiful moments, beautiful art, and timeless beauty in your home.

Note: It's okay to throw out photographs, especially ones that aren't particularly interesting or flattering. I threw out hundreds of my parents' photos, and there are still more than enough left to preserve family memories.

Family heirlooms

I mentioned family heirlooms earlier, but I think it's important to cover the topic further, especially when it comes to shifting a Yellow Zone to a Green Zone.

Family heirlooms can be a sensitive subject. If this is an issue for you, here is the bottom line: You have a choice about keeping or getting rid of inherited items. Antique stores and auction houses are filled with other people's family treasures ready for someone else to love!

Notice how you feel about family heirlooms that you have in your home. A friend of ours has a beautiful portrait of his great-grandmother on his wall. Once when we were visiting, I recognized the exceptional quality of the frame and painting and asked if his family had been wealthy. He explained, with surprising emotion, that, yes, the family had been quite wealthy at one time until the woman in the picture was widowed, made bad investments, and lost the family fortune. I asked him, if he was so upset with her, why did he have her picture on his wall? We laughed, but it did make me wonder about the underlying emotions that can accompany family heirlooms.

If you have inherited items in your home, ask yourself whether you are keeping them because you love and use them, or keeping them out of a sense of obligation. Look at what's in your home with discerning eyes.

Ask yourself:

- *Do I use this?*
- *Do I like it?*
- *Would I choose to have this in my home if it did not come from family?*

If you are keeping something only because it came to you as a gift or an inheritance, let it go. A client of ours kept a broken clock for over fifty years because it had been a wedding gift. You have absolute freedom to choose what you keep in your home. What are you keeping out of a sense of obligation?

Updating

You may have noticed that the years go by quickly. Notice as things around you at home get worn-out or become out-of-date. Look at the following:

- Paint colors
- Light fixtures
- Bedding
- Towels

- Window coverings
- Lamps
- Furniture
- Rugs
- Pots and pans, dishes, cutlery, and cooking utensils
- Details, such as floor vents, light switches, and door handles
- Mailbox
- And, well, everything…

Clear out everything that is worn or broken. You would be amazed at the pleasure that a new cookie sheet can bring! See what is in your cupboards and drawers simply by default. What is on your list of getting to "one day?"

When you replace items such as appliances, bathroom fixtures, window coverings, tiles, flooring, and major furniture, try to go classic and timeless in style. Save trendy choices for pillows, placemats, and other accessories that you change more often.

Paint color

I choose paint colors all the time for people who are selling their houses. That part is relatively easy, since people at that point are generally emotionally detached from their home. What has surprised me is how often clients have liked their new "show" colors so much that they decided to use the same ones in their next house. I don't have training as a color consultant, but I am very intuitive when it comes to choices like that. You can be, too, or maybe you already are.

Colors are very personal, so take time to notice what you like. Color carries energy, so choose your paint colors with care. Generally, it's best not to go too wild with color, unless that is very much a part of who you are, it's important to you, and you know what you are doing. My friend Carolyn has the most colorful house I have ever seen. She even has painted rugs on the floors and painted curtains around the windows. It is beautiful because she is a gifted artist, and it suits her uniquely. Few people could create what she has. Look around and find what feels right for you.

Paint colors evoke different emotional responses. For example, orange tones are supposed to be good for conversation, yellow for thinking, and red in the dining room stimulates appetite. Much information is available about the impact of paint color on living space, so do a bit of research. Painting your home in natural tones is a generally a good choice for creating a space that feels comfortable. If you have a high personal need for color, choose thoughtfully; think too about how you can express that need for color through art, area rugs and accessories.

Whatever colors you select, make your choice from a genuine desire to create a beautiful space. The most puzzling color selection I have seen was made by someone who explained to me that she had chosen bright yellow, orange, and blue intermingled out of a desire not to be boring. When I heard the motivation, I understood the result. Not wanting to be boring is a much different intention (and vibration) from wanting to create beauty.

Notice what emotion is driving your color choices in your home. Choose from a desire to create beauty, and you will be fine.

Even if you're comfortable choosing paint colors, it is often worth the effort to get a trained color consultant to help you. Paint colors can look very different in different environments, in different lights, and at different times of day. An hour or two with a professional can save you lots of time, money, and frustration.

If you are moving into a new space, it is generally best to re-paint, even if you like the existing colors. Paint holds the energy of the people who lived there previously, so unless your place was painted just before you moved in, it's best to start fresh.

Make sure that you are feeling calm and grounded when choosing paint colors so that you *feel* the colors. Getting the right color is as much an intuitive process as it is a visual one. Even if you work with a consultant, it can be worthwhile to get a sample to try on the wall. Whatever your process for selecting paint color, when you feel your "yes", get rolling!

> *"If I create from the heart, nearly everything works;*
> *if from the head, almost nothing."*
> —Marc Chagall

Sniff it out

The smells in your home are important; a Green Zone smells fresh and neutral, naturally. As a starting point, remove potentially toxic air fresheners, such as plug-in versions and sprays. I have noticed that I can tell when a house has plug-in air freshener within seconds of walking in or sometimes even before opening the door. I can feel a burning sensation when I breathe. The same with scented candles, unless they are non-toxic and naturally scented (the word "natural" on the package is not a guarantee). The best candles to use are natural beeswax, which actually help to improve air quality.

Be extra sensitive to pet smells. I have been in homes of people with cats and dogs where I couldn't detect a smell and others where a pungent odor hit me at the front threshold. If you have pets, keep them clean and well-groomed. Keep pet food well sealed. Have carpets cleaned regularly. When the weather suits, open windows to let fresh air flow through. If you are unsure if your house passes a "sniff test", ask a friend to give you an honest opinion.

Another factor in your indoor air quality is your furnace. It is a good idea to have your furnace checked and cleaned annually, and to change furnace filters regularly. We have seen furnace filters that have not been changed in years, sometimes because people didn't even know they had them. Dirty furnace filters make the air in your home unhealthy, and put stress on your furnace. Advice on how often you need to change filters varies – check the recommendations for your furnace.

Let there be light

It is worth emphasizing here the difference that light can make in how your home feels, and how you feel. As you go through your home, check to see where you can benefit from adding lamps, or increasing the wattage in existing lamps and light fixtures. You will be amazed at the positive impact additional light can have on a room. Dimmer switches and tri-lights are great for adding flexibility. Check window coverings to make sure they open and close easily to allow natural light in when you want it.

Home maintenance

Much of what needs to be done when people are getting their houses ready to sell, quite honestly, is home maintenance that really needed to be done all along—also called "deferred maintenance." If you are a homeowner, whether you are selling your house or not, it is in your best interest to make sure that your roof is in good condition, to keep your eaves or gutters clear and positioned to direct water away from your home, and make sure window and door trim is repainted or re-sealed periodically.

Make sure that all electrical work meets safety code. There are hundreds of details to home maintenance, but if you raise your Awareness of what needs to be attended to in your home, and keep up with it, it will serve you and your home. Whatever the cost of good maintenance, it is less than the cost of ignoring things and having to do major repairs down the road.

Note: If you are not a homeowner, you will benefit from treating your property with the same care as if you owned it. Nudge your landlord to keep on top of maintenance when necessary, including re-painting where reasonably warranted.

Have fun. Take your time. Notice if you feel frustrated, overwhelmed, or self-critical along the way. Updating your home is not about feeling that you should have done something sooner; it's about seeing what you can choose for yourself, now. When you see something you want to change, it means you have expanded your Awareness. When you expand your Awareness while feeling excited, hopeful, or curious (or any of the other receptive emotions), your Desire and Willingness are guaranteed to follow!

Note: Please, if your finances are stressed right now, steer your thoughts away from worry or lack. Do what you can, think about what you would like to do, and practice feeling grateful in advance for everything that is coming to you. You will be amazed at what can shift when you let go of fear and worry.

Quality is worth the search

Whatever items you are looking to purchase for your home, take the time you need to find things you love, and enjoy the search. Buying good quality is important. Good quality carries a vibration that you can feel. Take particular care in choosing longer-life items, especially the 3 Fs: furniture, flooring, and fixtures. Good quality does not have to equal expensive; you will always be able to find a good sale or well-priced options. Good quality items stay looking good much longer.

Delight in the search and don't rush yourself into a decision. You will learn so much about what is available and what you like. At the same time, don't obsess about your choices. Go easy and have some fun. Recognize that your tastes may have changed in the past few years and be open to new ideas. You might be surprised at what styles you gravitate toward now.

Affirmations to shift a Yellow Zone

- *I welcome new things into my life.*
- *I love to learn.*
- *I am creating a rich and vibrant life.*
- *I am willing to release what no longer serves me.*
- *I express myself with confidence and ease.*
- *I am worthy of beauty.*
- *I am ready to move forward.*
- *I am ready to rock my life.*

Actions to jump-start you from a Yellow Zone

First, ask yourself: "Does this space make me feel excited about the 'me' I want to become and the life I want to live?"

Learn to notice what's around you. Get excited when you see something you want to change. Remember, your goal is to develop unconscious Awareness, from which you can be observant and "in the moment" at the same time. Cultivate a gentle Awareness that allows your intuitive side to come through. See the details of your home in a way that sparks Desires that light you up.

Keep a list. What would you like? Write down everything that comes to mind, even if it's just a little detail.

Exercise for creating a jump-start

Look around your home and notice five small things that are worn-out, out-of-date, or just not what you like. They should be things that are easily within your financial means to replace. They can include anything: a spatula, a set of measuring spoons, a tea towel, a frying pan, clothes hangers for your closet, a bath towel, or even a toilet brush or a laundry basket: it doesn't matter what the items are, but be specific.

1. _____
2. _____
3. _____
4. _____
5. _____

For the next five weeks, pick one item a week, and go out and buy yourself a replacement that you really like. Look around, consider the different features and options available to you, and choose an item that you are really pleased with. Delight in the details that you notice. Yes, even a new toilet brush can be exciting! It is amazing how many different choices there are. The point of the exercise is to help you develop the habit of noticing the details of your home and how good it feels to change them.

Note: When you buy a new item, be sure to get rid of the old one!

Does your home support spontaneity?

One benefit of living in Receiving Condition is being able to welcome people into your home easily. If your doorbell rang right now, would you be able to receive unexpected guests in a style you would feel good about?

Here are a few tips to be able to receive guests at a moment's notice:

• Keep all surfaces, such as counters and tables, clean, especially in the kitchen, bathroom and living areas.
• Keep floor areas clear of anything other than furniture and lamps and accessories.
• Make cleaning and tidying a daily practice: a minute here and a minute there make a huge difference.

- Include your porch, and pay special attention to entrance areas.
- Keep some basic drinks and snacks on hand—just in case.

These daily practices are not about what surprise guests think of you; they are about aligning the energy in your home to attract and welcome good experiences. Guests or no guests, it is always in your best interest to have a clean, tidy, welcoming home.

As you observe what is in your home, ask yourself:

- Does this space feel good? Does this space feel right?
- Is this the kitchen of people who are taking good care of themselves?
- Is this the bathroom of people who nurture themselves?
- Is this the home of people who appreciate and welcome beauty?

To shift a Yellow Zone to Green, consider the following questions?

- Where in your home are you in limbo?
- Where in your home are you "tolerating?"
- Where in your home are you "settling?"
- Where in your home are you "resigned?"

Now, if you really want to create a shift, consider:

- Where in your *life* are you holding back?
- Where in your *life* are you in limbo?
- Where in your *life* are you "tolerating?"
- Where in your *life* are you "settling?"
- Where in your *life* are you "resigned?"

Notice how things shift in your life as you make changes in your home.

Amplify your Awareness and Desire by shopping!

Despite the fact that shopping has become an addiction for some people in our culture, shopping with the intention to expand your Awareness and Desire can be healthy and helpful. The kind of shopping I am talking about doesn't even necessarily include a purchase. By nature, your Desires are limited to what you already know exists or can imagine, right? If you take the time to look around at what is available, you can discover options you didn't know existed. If you don't like to shop, try to find some way to enjoy it, even if it's only to expand your Awareness of your choices. If you have a strong aversion to shopping in stores, you can use your computer to get ideas without even leaving home.

If you don't want to look around because you can't afford to buy anything right now, you have an opportunity for a breakthrough around money issues. If you can get to the point where you feel genuinely excited about what is out there for you even before you have the money to buy it, you will experience a shift in energy. You have to feel good about money *before* you have it. Get out there and look, and let yourself feel as though you can buy anything you want!

Note: We will look at how to release money issues shortly.

Tips for happy shopping

- Be sure you are hydrated, fed, and rested before you go out.
- Shop alone if you can, at least in the beginning. If you have a partner who is making decisions with you, make final major purchases together, but start looking on your own.
- Unless you are absolutely certain of your purchase, buy only in stores that offer a full refund on returns. Even professional designers can't always tell how things are going to look at home.
- If you look around and still don't find anything you like, trust that the best option is still out there. Relax and take your time.

A few places to find inspiration

Real Estate Open Houses——Don't be shy about going to a real estate Open House, even if you have no intention of buying a new home. This is a great way to get ideas for décor and use of space. Realtors welcome people to their Open Houses.

Local Home Shows——Most major cities have at least one consumer Home Show a year where you can see the latest in home renovation and decoration ideas, all under one roof. Check to see if one is scheduled near you.

Retail Stores and Showrooms——Go out, wander the stores, and have some fun. Often designer or furniture shops are clustered close together so you don't have to go too far. Go beyond the mainstream or big box stores, although they can be good resources too; have a look at some of the higher-end or boutique stores to find ideas. Looking around can give you creative ideas, and sometimes it simply helps you appreciate what you already have.

Books and Magazines——Designer books and magazines can be a big help in giving you inspiration and ideas. Look at the pictures in detail. You might see ideas for bedding, window coverings, furniture, table settings, a rug, a lamp, or any number of items. The advertisements in magazines can also be helpful. Before you purchase books or magazines, check your local library to see what is available for free.

Television Programs——It seems there are new design shows on television every week. Some programs are quite helpful and inspiring, but recognize that just because a design idea is on television does not guarantee that it is a good one! Use your own discernment.

The World Wide Web——You have an endless resource at your fingertips to help with any question about the details of your home. Use the Internet to help you to source and price specific items that you have in mind.

Other People's Houses——Start to notice the details of other people's houses when you visit. You never know where you will find ideas or inspiration.

Sometimes the perfect item finds you! Trust!

I had been looking for throw pillows for our living room couch for a long time. My husband and I attended a charity silent auction where I saw two beautiful designer oversized pillows that I knew would be perfect. I hovered around those pillows all night and put in a higher bid whenever I needed to. At the very last second, someone else scooped up the pillows. A couple of days later, I got a call asking if I was still interested in buying them. It turns out the pillows didn't look good in the top bidder's house—but they look great in ours!

Have fun noticing how the perfect things can just show up in your life when your energy is aligned to what you want!

If you just can't get excited about "stuff"

If you genuinely don't like to shop, or if you don't get excited about material possessions, relax. You do not have to covet material possessions for HouseHeal to make a difference in your life. Material accumulation is not what Receiving Condition is about. You can live very happily without vast or luxurious possessions. At the same time, no matter how spiritual you are, you live in a physical world, and there can be great joy in experiencing the comfort and convenience that is available to you, on whatever scale works for you.

It is exceedingly rare for a person who is living from a place of love and happiness to have anything but appreciation for the physical comforts and conveniences of life, and for a beautiful living space. One client sold his beautifully cared-for house and gave up his personal material possessions to become a Buddhist monk. Even though he now has no income, and certainly does not covet material possessions, he still lives in clean, peaceful, beautiful surroundings that support him in living a life he loves.

Beauty can be simple. It is up to you to choose what feels right to you. If you are uncomfortable about expressing your Desires, you may need to release some limiting beliefs in order to explore and experience what is available to you.

Opt for service or experiences over stuff

If your list of "stuff" is pretty much complete for the moment and you are happy with your home and how you feel there, that's great. To keep the energy moving, maybe consider services or experiences that would enhance your life. Would you like to hire a gardener, have someone deliver home-cooked meals, do your laundry, or even have part-time personal assistant? Go ahead and dream about what kind of help and services you would like. What about experiences? Maybe there are family members or friends that you would like to have come to visit, or maybe you would like time alone to sit and read a good book or take a long bath. Maybe you want to host a dinner party, do flower arranging, play the piano, garden or learn to sew. Let your mind scroll through the possibilities. The more you expand your Desires in a way that feels real and exciting, the more you will be pulled forward.

Recognize that Yellow to Green is a big personal shift

When you become aware of your Yellow Zones and take steps to shift them, you will notice all kinds of changes within and around you. Shifting a Yellow Zone to Green goes far beyond what is physically in your home. This process is about you choosing what is best for you at home, and consciously and continuously taking good care of yourself, doing everything in your power to create a life that you love! That's big, so give yourself proper credit for making the shift.

Chapter Eight
Maintaining and Expanding a Green Zone

You might think that once you achieve your Green Zones, life becomes a breeze. It's not quite that simple. Remember, maintaining and expanding your Green Zones requires constant care and attention to detail. Just because you have identified an area as Green doesn't mean it can't get even better and expand. It also doesn't mean that it is guaranteed to stay Green. Things in any home, no matter how beautiful and well-maintained, eventually get tired and outdated. Life changes. Your perception of yourself and your home changes. Your needs change. Your Awareness and Desire shift.

When my husband and I bought our current house, we lived in our basement for six months while we renovated. When we finally moved upstairs, every square inch of the house was a Green Zone to me, no matter what remained to be finished. Now, ten years later, I look around and still see Green Zones, but because of time and new projects (expanded Desire!), I see bigger areas of Yellow. There is still movement in our house, slowly but surely, so I know that the Yellow Zones are gradually shifting to Green. Movement is the key to expanding and strengthening Green Zones in your home.

Take pleasure in the areas of your home that you have identified as Green Zones and be grateful for them. Be open to inspiration for making the space even richer in detailed beauty and function.

Guidelines for maintaining and expanding a Green Zone

- Be vigilant with items that quickly clutter space, such as paper, books, and magazines. Clean and tidy are essential components of Green Zones.
- Notice when things in your home start to show wear and update them as needed. Enjoy the process of looking for new things that you love, and trust the right inspiration will come to you.
- Remember that a Green Zone needs happy activity to feel alive—a dining room without happy gatherings, a bedroom without good sleep, or a living room without good conversation won't stay Green in vibration very long, no matter how beautiful.
- Set yourself up for zero-stress—keep groceries stocked, maintain a good supply of laundry detergent, dishwashing soap, shampoos, deodorant and other essential personal products, keep back-ups of all household items that could cause stress if they suddenly ran out—batteries for smoke detectors and remote control units; light bulbs, especially specialty bulbs that are hard to find; toilet paper; and if you have a home office, toner and paper for your printer. A Green Zone is filled with a sense of ease.
- Remain open to new ideas and inspiration. Even when what you have is beautiful, sometimes as you raise your vibration, something else becomes a better match to you. Notice when what you have is no longer your taste (furniture, paint color, bedding, etc.) and be willing to make changes that feel right.
- Buy only things that you love, or that give you that "yes" feeling.
- Think conscious thoughts of appreciation for your Green Zones— notice what you love around you and say thank you, every day.

Affirmations for maintaining and strengthening your Green Zones

Here are just a few examples:
- *I appreciate the details of my home and enjoy caring for them.*
- *I am safe and loved.*
- *I nurture myself daily.*
- *I accept my power to choose what is in my home.*

- *My home supports me in everything I do.*
- *My home is filled with ever-expanding love and beauty.*
- *My home is my foundation for more and more good things in my life.*
- *I am open to receiving all good things at home.*
- *I live from love.*
- *I am grateful for my home and my life. Thank you!*

Write some affirmations that work for you. Remember, words alone are not enough. To make affirmations effective, you need words *and* feeling together.

Purchase only what truly calls to you

Green Zones demand that you be selective with what you bring into your space. I like to use an "overnight test" for purchases that I am not quite sure about or for anything I cannot return. If I see something I like but have even the slightest hesitation about buying it, I leave it to sit overnight, or longer, and accept that it might be gone. If the item haunts me, I go back and buy it. If it leaves my thoughts, I forget about it. This strategy pays off.

One Fall weekend a few years ago, my husband and I went for a drive in the country and stumbled upon a one-month garage sale on the main street of a small town. A retired geologist had been instructed by his wife to reduce the "stuff" he had gathered through his travels over the years. He came up with the brilliant idea of renting an empty store for a month.

The man's collection included some beautiful hand-made statues of Magi, each carrying a small pot for flammable oil. Each statue was unique in detail and had been made by a French artist who had died some years before. The man told us that he had loved the statues so much that he bought all the artist had. My husband encouraged me to buy one, but at the time, I was trying very hard not to spend any money. I insisted that if I wanted one badly enough I could drive back to the shop before the end of the month.

I forgot about the statues until the very last day of the month, when suddenly I sat bolt upright in bed and told my husband we had to go back. When we pulled up in front of the shop, I almost cried. The garage sale was gone, and renovations were underway for new law offices. A construction worker there remembered a man packing statues, so my hope was restored.

We asked around at the surrounding shops, but no one could help us. The florist next door recalled only that the man drove a big, old beige car and lived on the edge of town. She suggested that we head out on the main street, turn left over the railroad tracks, watch for a small street on the right, and keep our eyes open for his car.

We followed our few clues, and as we turned onto a little street on the edge of town, there, like a beacon, was a big, old beige car in a driveway. The man was just opening his garage door. I couldn't believe it. When the man took his six remaining statues of the Magi out of a box to show me, he arranged them by size on the hood of his car, in two groups of three. Suddenly I saw what I had missed the first time. There were *three* wise men, of course! I needed to get three of the magi statues, not just one.

Those Magi statues are among my favorite things today. I know that the reason I didn't buy one the first time was because I was meant to have three. I can't help but wonder if the other three Magi are still in a box in that man's garage.

Original art: a powerful way to raise your home's vibration

Original art has a vibration or energy that is different from anything mechanically mass-produced. Original art changes the feel of a home. You do not have to be an expert to buy original art. You just have to know what you like.

Look for local art shows—or take an art class. Check out local art galleries just to get a feel for what you like. I mean that literally. If you are grounded and connected, you will be able to *feel* the art.

Art does not have to come with a big price tag. When I was growing up, my parents had a big painting in their living room, a big white canvas with red and blue abstract shapes. A friend of the family had done the painting in only minutes, just to have something to hang on the wall. I don't know where that painting is now, but I remember it being as nice as many works I have seen in modern art museums. Be creative and resourceful. Maybe you have children who can help to create some of the art in your home.

Personally, I am a fan of big pieces. We have several paintings in our house that are three feet by four feet and larger. And we do not live in a big house. I bought at least two of the paintings when I had next to no money and paid the artist in installments. There are many artists who are happy to have people appreciate their work and who sell their paintings at very reasonable prices.

Have fun looking and discovering what you like. Do you want an abstract? A landscape? Don't be afraid to go for big pieces if you like them.

If you already have original art in your home, look at what you have and think, "What next?" You might even see that some pieces no longer resonate with you the way they did when you bought them. If that happens, you might decide to sell them and buy something that fits you and your home at this time.

Buy paintings from love and an appreciation of beauty, and you will make good choices.

As you look around at art, you will find that you connect with certain pieces. I fell in love with a painting at an artist friend's show but at the time I did not have the money to buy it. My friend knew how I much I loved the painting; she even made me a beautiful miniature of it for Christmas. Months later, the painting came suddenly to my thoughts and I e-mailed my friend to see if it was still for sale. She replied that someone had put a hold on the painting just the day before. When the other buyer heard how much I wanted the piece, he graciously released it. Even though I had not thought of the painting for months, when someone else was about to buy it, it was as if it called out to me. By then, oddly enough, I had the money to buy it.

Listen to what's in your home

Sound is vibration. Listen to the sounds in your home. Sound can be uplifting or it can contribute to your stress level. We live in an age of electronics: televisions, computers, radios, games, and music. Notice whether you are on sound overload in your house and learn to enjoy occasional silence.

Notice the music you are playing. Does it help you feel good? Does it make you feel happy, relaxed, energized, uplifted, or however you want to feel in that moment? Is your music current or do you play old songs all the time? Remember, just like inherited items and old photos, old music can keep you stuck in the past, too! We all love our "oldies" weekends on the radio, but make an effort to discover some of the brilliant new music that is coming out every day.

Maybe your house is too quiet and would benefit from more music.

Maybe you and your house need more quiet time.

Do a "sound check" to make sure that what you are listening to, for the most part at least, helps raise the vibration of your home, not lower it.

Healthy Awareness is vital to a Green Zone

Remember this?

OBLIVIOUS ⇐	Aware/Intentional/Active	⇒ OBSESSIVE
(unhealthy)	(healthy)	(unhealthy)

Stay in healthy Awareness and make it part of how you live. If you retreat into being oblivious in your Green Zones, they will shift to Yellow over time. On the other hand, if you obsess about maintaining your Green Zones, the energy of fear or worry will bring the energy to Yellow. Learn to keep a healthy level of Awareness, largely unconscious, that will help you to maintain daily attention to detail and to make changes as needed, yet at the same time relax and enjoy your home – and maybe even allow yourself to be messy on brief occasions!

A Green Zone cannot be purchased

Green Zones can be enhanced by what you purchase, certainly, but most important is to fill your Green Zones with happy, loving thoughts and activities. The vital essence of a Green Zone, its vibration, originates within you.

Chapter Nine
People, Money, and Thoughts

Other people in your home

Here's the part you've been waiting for, right? Other people!

Here's the deal, like it or not: The people you live with contribute to the vibration of your home, but they are not an excuse for delaying action in your home. Living with other people—spouses, children, parents, and roommates—comes with its challenges and lessons, but if you believe that other people are the main problem in your home, you are in for a surprise.

We all attract people into our lives to reveal what we need to learn about ourselves. If you are feeling frustrated, angry, or any other resistant emotion connected to your home and the people in it, take a deep breath. Examine what is at the heart of that emotion and see what needs to be healed. Here's a hint: It is always about you.

Your emotional upset in any situation is never really about the other person. Even if you are certain that the other person is the cause of the mess, chaos, décor, disrepair, or inertia in your home, your own emotional upset about your home is always related to you and to how you feel about *you*. It's always about you. Even when your complaints seem real and justified, even if people you live with are lazy, unreasonable, or whatever else, and even when your friends agree with you that it's not your fault, it is about you. When you are willing to look, you will always find the actual root of your issues inside.

If you feel frustrated with another person, you are actually frustrated with yourself. If you think you are angry with someone else, you are actually angry with yourself. Emotional upset at another person always originates within you.

Maybe you are frustrated that you have not created more money in your life. Maybe you are mad at yourself for not having better boundaries and for not looking after your own needs better. Maybe you are frustrated with yourself for not speaking up about what is important to you. Maybe you are mad at yourself for not doing what you really want. Maybe you are upset for failing to make choices that, deep down, you know would be best for you.

You can find the root of every upset if you are willing to look in the mirror. This does not mean it's your fault. It does not mean that other people's behavior isn't sometimes genuinely frustrating. It just means that your emotional response is within your control, and that is a good thing.

Let me be clear: other people's energy definitely affects you and your home. And yes, it can be challenging to live with someone who is messy, lazy, noisy, or whatever. It's just that when you become aware and engage in your own healing, other people have less and less power over you, even the people closest to you—the ones you live with. Typically, as you change your overall emotions to a more receptive vibration, the people around you change, too, without much effort on your part.

The lesson here is that people will only annoy, frustrate, or anger you to the degree that there is something in *you* that would be helpful for you to recognize and release.

> *"No one saves us but ourselves. No one can and no one may. We ourselves must walk the path."*
> —Hindu Prince Gautama Siddharta, the founder of Buddhism, 563-483 B.C.

Notice where you are waiting for others to take action.

I was visiting a friend and noticed that her kitchen cabinets had mismatched handles, most of them old and unattractive. She told me that she wanted to replace them and some time ago had asked her husband to look after that job. She was obviously frustrated that he hadn't done it. I suggested that we go out immediately and get new hardware. Within an hour, and for relatively little money, we had bought and installed all-new matching handles on her cabinets. It was an instant transformation. She was relieved and happy, and so was her husband. Problem solved.

Like it or not, you create your own experiences at home. You choose your thoughts and your words. You choose your emotional response in every situation.

If you want other people to change, change your thoughts about those people. The people may or may not change their behavior, but the dynamic between you will shift. You have the power to influence your relationships with other people just by taking charge of your own life and shifting your own vibration. If you respond from a place of love and compassion in any situation, you will make a good choice.

Act from love

Remember, act only from a place of feeling good. When you notice yourself experiencing negative or resistant emotions, stop for a minute. Do not speak, e-mail, blog, phone, drive, or shop online—Do *nothing*! Trust me on this. I have had moments of acting like a crazy person which I could have avoided had I followed my own advice! Notice and start to think yourself into thoughts that feel better *before* you take action and potentially cause yourself and others harm.

Not taking action does not mean holding back your emotions

Please understand: not taking action does not mean that you don't express emotions. Expressing your emotions is necessary and healthy. Some of the most positive shifts in my home and marriage have come after I "let it out" with full emotion. Not with meanness, but with in-the-moment, emotional truth about what I was and was not willing to accept and what was important to me.

There is a difference between emotional expression and emotional assault. When you are expressing yourself from your true emotions (receptive energy) rather than from temporary insanity (resistant energy), time will not change what you have to say. If you feel intense, overwhelming emotion, wait a bit before you speak. And definitely wait before you act. If what you have to say is really your truth, it will still be there for you to express a little later when you feel calmer.

Set boundaries, even with people you love

When it comes to other people, you have a choice about who comes to your home—even family and friends. You have the right to protect the good energy in your home, but protect it with kindness and love. If there are people in your life whose energy brings you down, you can choose not to have them in your home as long as you do it from a place of love. Often, you don't even need to announce it. You can simply choose, politely, to be unavailable to get together or suggest that you meet somewhere else instead of your home. You will find that as you raise your vibration, some people will naturally become less a part of your life, and new people will appear, and that's okay.

When you feel you have no choice about the guest list, such as when hosting a holiday, birthday, or traditional gathering where you are obliged to include certain people that you find difficult, decide in advance that you are not going to let them "push your buttons." Think kind thoughts about them before they arrive, and make an extra effort to keep your thoughts in check during the festivities.

If you can, try to get to the underlying cause of your emotional buttons. If someone pushes your buttons, it's because you have the buttons to push in the first place. Notice where you get hooked. The good news is, as you do this work and release your emotional blocks, fewer and fewer people will be able to push your buttons.

Even with family, you have a choice. Once, my brother was coming to stay at our house when there was still an unresolved issue with our mother's estate. I called him and told him nicely that if the issue wasn't resolved for him, I couldn't have him stay at our house. I just didn't want to bring that unsettled energy and the inevitable discussions into my peaceful home. Because I spoke honestly and from my heart, he understood. We resolved things, and our relationship was not only unharmed, it became closer on some levels.

Making decisions as a couple is important

As hard as it may be sometimes, it is important for couples to make significant decisions about home together. You can choose to defer to your partner for some decisions, of course, and vice versa, but only if that deferral is given freely, with awareness, love, and respect, and not in a spirit of resignation or resentment. There are horror stories of couples who fight while doing renovations together, but that doesn't need to be the case. My husband and I have been through two major renovations and more, and we have found that we make better decisions together than either of us would make on our own. We often have our differences, but it works.

One thing has helped us: we have an agreement in which we both have veto power on any choice or decision, no explanation necessary. "No, I don't like that," is enough. We work on the premise that if we really listen to each other and respect each other's opinions, we will be able to find something that we both like even when we don't agree at the start.

One recent example was when we had the front porch rebuilt on our hundred-year-old house. When it came time to replace our worn-out concrete steps, my husband wanted traditional wooden steps, and I wanted something more solid and substantial. My husband said he absolutely did not want concrete steps, and I absolutely did not want wooden ones. We were at a standstill. When I told our designer about our dilemma, he suggested natural stone steps, which we hadn't even thought of. We both loved the idea; it addressed both of our concerns. People walk past our house now and call out to tell us that they love our front steps—and we do, too!

Emotional upset: one at a time, please

The first person to get upset has dibs. Try it. It works miracles. Making up this rule has dramatically reduced the number of disagreements in our house. It's simple. Both partners agree that if somebody gets upset, the other one stays calm. No engaging, no cajoling, no trying to reason, just staying calm and quiet. Give the other person space to let it out. If two people get upset at the same time, emotions escalate in the wrong direction. If only one person gets upset at time, the upset won't go very far.

It's very important to understand that another person's emotional upset has nothing to do with you. If you know this, it is easier to come from kindness and compassion. Even when your partner (or friend, family member, or even a stranger) appears to be upset with you, understand that it is not really about you. Don't take it personally. Whatever it is, it's about something inside them. It is not about you, I promise. Stay calm and send love.

Note: This rule is meant for a relatively normal level of emotional upset. Abusive language and behavior from anyone, especially a partner, is not acceptable. Learn to recognize the difference between emotional upset and abuse, and do not tolerate abuse.

> *"When you know better you do better."*
> —Maya Angelou

Be mindful of your thoughts about other people

People feel your thoughts and are affected by them, even if they don't consciously hear them, especially at home. Negative or critical thoughts are like heat-seeking missiles aimed at the person you are thinking about, and they are missiles that boomerang back at you. If you have negative thoughts about someone, stop immediately and direct your thoughts somewhere else. Do not inflict negative energy on others. Please. It hurts them, and it hurts you. Make an effort to fill your home with kind thoughts.

When I was taking my "mind power" course many years ago, each week I mailed a photocopy of my notes to my mother, who read them faithfully. My mother called me one day to say that she had done one of the weekly exercises and had startling results.

The exercise in my course notes was to stop and notice how you were feeling, then to notice what you were thinking, and then to become aware of the connection between your thoughts and feelings. The next step was to replace negative thoughts with positive thoughts and notice the difference in how you felt. My mother told me that, when she did the exercise, she noticed that she had been sitting there thinking nasty, critical thoughts about my father. When she saw what she was doing, right away she switched her thoughts to focus on the genuinely nice things about my father. She noticed an immediate change in her feelings toward him.

Then came the amazing part. My father walked into the room and within a few minutes asked my mother, "What's different with you?" He had noticed a difference in the "vibration" coming from my mother that quickly, just from her shifting her thoughts. The energy between my parents changed instantly when my mother consciously altered her thoughts about my father. My mother told me it was a pivotal moment in their marriage.

Several years later, when my mother was dying and reflecting on her forty-six years with my father, she said to me quite proudly and lovingly, "You know, your father and I had fourteen really good years together."

My brothers, sisters, and I had a good chuckle at that one. Perhaps fourteen out of forty-six isn't something to aspire to, but I knew what she meant. And I know that most, if not all, of the happiest years of my parents' marriage came after my mother became aware of the power of her thoughts. When you think genuine thoughts of love, it changes everything.

Children know

Children notice and appreciate order and beauty. Over the years, I have been amazed at the phone calls I have received from parents telling me how much their children loved what we did in their rooms during the "prep to sell" process. Many times, parents have gone out to replicate the pieces their children loved, from rugs to lamps to pictures. Once when we were packing up a house, my instinct told me to leave a rug I had bought for a little girl's room. Instead of following my intuition, I rationalized that if I left something behind at every house, it would become a big expense over the year. Just when our moving truck was about to leave the driveway, the little girl arrived home from school. She hurried up to me and, looking up at me with big eyes, asked if she could buy the rug that was in her room. I just about melted. I took the rug out of the truck and gave it to her. Her parents told me she planned her whole room in the new house around that rug.

Kids don't have to equal chaos

Kids are messy, for sure. But they can learn just as easily as adults, perhaps even more easily, that a clean and tidy living environment feels better than a dirty, messy one. It is helpful for kids to learn to contain their mess and to tidy up one mess before they start on the next one. This is not meant to create stress in the house around enforced tidiness or to stifle the freedom and pleasure of play. It is merely meant to encourage cleaning up messes regularly for everyone's sake. Remember: the longer the mess stays, the heavier the energy gets. Keep things moving.

And, yes, it is possible for kids to learn to tidy up after themselves. I have witnessed it many times. My nephew came to visit our house shortly after his mother had read the draft of this book and began to apply its concepts. For the first time, my nephew cleaned up and put away the Jenga blocks before he came upstairs for bed—without being asked. I was amazed, and he was pleased. Notice your thoughts and beliefs about kids and mess. Your kids just might surprise you.

Trust that other people are on their right path

If you know other people who can benefit from HouseHeal, go ahead and recommend this book enthusiastically, tell everyone you know, give copies to your friends and family along with a nudge of encouragement, share your experiences and send inspiring messages out through your social networks—please do!—and then trust that other people will be moved to action when they are ready. It's great to be encouraging and enthusiastic, and you can make a big difference to people's lives by sharing. Just do your best to be unattached to who takes action. Everyone has their own timing.

Envy no one

Take care not to compare your home to anyone else's. You are not in a contest with family, friends, neighbors, co-workers, or strangers to see who has the nicest home. The person whose home and life you envy may well be envying you. The person with the beautiful house and perfect-looking life may be deeply unhappy. There is no one way that happiness looks. You need to choose your happiness for you, without comparing yourself to anyone else.

Money is great, but happiness first!

It is easy to tell yourself that your house or your life is stuck because you lack money. Lack of money is never the real issue. Winning the lottery is not the answer to your problems. In fact, several documentaries have been made about lottery winners who were broke and miserable before they won millions and who returned to being broke and miserable after their windfall. That's because they remained vibrationally matched to being broke.

Lack of money can feel like an all-consuming problem, but it is really a *symptom* of blocked energy and limiting beliefs. Lack of money is an indication that you are missing something in the process of Awareness, Desire, and Willingness. If you want to be happy and have more money flow into your life, you need to feel good about money *before* you have it. In fact, unless you feel good about money now, you will never feel like you have enough of it, even when you actually have it.

Feeling like you have money is a healthy and powerful practice, but it does not mean that you spend money you do not have; it means staying in the energy of "all is well" and taking all of the right action possible within your circumstances. In fact, consciously choosing *not* to spend money can feel wonderful and empowering.

Notice your thoughts about money

Notice the difference between how these two statements feel:
I can't spend any money right now. (powerless)
I choose not to spend money right now. (powerful)
Even without money, you can do lots to raise the vibration of your home and change your energetic point of attraction. In fact, the most important part of shifting your energy—thinking thoughts that help you feel better—is free. Loving, creative, hopeful thoughts are yours to choose any time you want them—at no charge. Many actions that help to generate a receptive vibration in your home, such as tidying, purging, cleaning, and de-cluttering, are also free.

Take action in your home with the resources you have right now and *feel* as though money is flowing to you. Think uplifting thoughts. Let your frustrations out if you need to. Remember to ground and connect every day. Do everything you can, right now, and *know* deep within you that good things are already yours and are on their way to you.

Do not let a lack of money prevent you from taking action and loving your life. Get happy in your thoughts and feelings first, take action, and notice how quickly things in your life change.

Affirmations

Try this affirmation:

Money flows to me faster and faster as I release my frustrations and fears. I am grateful for all that I have, and for all that is coming to me now.

Or write your own affirmation:

_____

_____

_____

Decide to be happy

When you decide to feel happy, you will find that money and everything else you want will flow to you more easily. If you focus too much on money as your goal, you will find that money alone does not bring happiness. Pay sufficient attention to your money that you pay your bills on time and make responsible choices, but do not obsess. As much as we all enjoy having money, money does not guarantee a life you love.

I was unhappy and financially strained for many years, and even though my money issues were stressful, no amount of money would have fixed my unhappiness for me. I had to find my happiness from within. Now that I am happier, more money is flowing to me each year.

That's what I want for myself: happiness and money flowing at the same time and living from a place of love. I hope it's what you want for yourself, too.

If it feels like you're trying to "fix" something, stop

Willingness comes from the desire to create. Trying to *fix* something in your home (or life) carries the vibration of "something is wrong." Trying to *create* something in your home (or life) carries the vibration of "something is possible." Guess which one is more powerful for creating the vibration of Receiving Condition?

Note: Here, *fixing* refers to an overall space or a situation, not to fixing something specific that is in disrepair, like a leaking faucet. If something in your home is in disrepair, fix away!

Drama equals resistance

Drama happens in your home when you allow resistant emotions to take over as if they were reality. Resistant emotions (anger, frustration, guilt, etc.) take up energetic space in your home, as much as furniture or other "stuff." If you want to live in Receiving Condition, be willing to let go of the drama in your life.

How do you reduce emotional drama in your home?

- Stay in present time. Do not bring up stories of hurt, anger, regret, frustration, or guilt from the past, especially if you are upset.
    Q: How can you tell if you are still emotionally hooked on the past?
    A: If you are still telling the story, you're still hooked.
- Follow the one-at-a-time rule. Do not engage with an upset person. Do your best to see others in your home with kindness and compassion.
- Remind yourself that the truth feels good. Emotional upset arises when you believe something negative that isn't true. Look for a new perspective that feels better.
- As best as you can make sure that you and other people in your home get enough sleep, good food, and water. Tired, hungry, dehydrated people get upset more easily.
- Keep your home clean and tidy to reduce stress.

"Just the way things are"

Let go of beliefs like, "That's just the way I am" or "That's just the way things are." It's simply not true. If you think you were born naturally messy, think again. When my husband and I were first together, I was messy, and he was neat to the extreme. It was challenging for both of us. I felt stressed and inadequate, and he was frustrated with my mess. Over time, we have been able to balance each other out. Now we have a mutual need for neatness, combined with a healthy tolerance for mess. We have both been able to change.

The biggest lie you will ever tell yourself is, "I have no choice."

Write it out

A good way to release emotion is to write it out. Get your feelings out and on paper. Just let it out, however it comes, taking as many pages as you need. When you finish writing, say thank you for the release, and then shred or safely burn what you have written. Let it go.

Speak it out—alone

If you have a private space, you might find it helps to talk aloud as a release. Talk to the Universe, to God, to your Guardian Angel, yourself, or to no one in particular—whatever you are comfortable with. This is one time when you don't need to worry about being negative or sounding strange—just let it all out with full emotion until you start to feel the shift in your body as you start to feel better. Say thank you and let it go.

Notice and appreciate the little differences

Have fun noticing the changes in your life as the energy in your home shifts. You might notice that you feel more relaxed. Maybe you will have more houseguests—or fewer! Maybe you will find yourself singing for no particular reason. Maybe you will sleep better, eat better, or have a higher energy level. Maybe you will start getting little tasks around the house completed more easily. Maybe you will notice that you are sitting down to dinner more often. Maybe you will experience more romance.

The changes may come slowly or quickly. They may be dramatic or subtle. But if you engage in the process as outlined here, the changes will come.

Putting the "heal" in HouseHeal

Clearing what's in your house, both physically and energetically, can stir up emotions. Take good care of yourself. Take warm baths. Move your body or be still. Notice what feels good. Sleep when you need to. Cry when you need to. Stretch your body. Know that you will never get this work all finished. There will always be something new to release, physically and emotionally. If you feel emotionally overwhelmed or stuck, you may want to consider getting some help to take the next step forward. There are many wonderful energy healers and healing modalities available these days to help you clear emotional blocks that you just can't get to on your own. Do research, ask around for personal referrals, and use your intuition to help you discern which method and practitioner is best for you at any given time. Keep in mind that even when working with a gifted healing practitioner, you need to be open and willing to receive the healing in order to benefit. At the same time, when you are given advice from anyone, check in with your intuition and follow what feels right to you.

How to know when you are putting The 3 Keys into practice

Here are some good indicators that you are practicing The 3 Keys and are well on your way to living in Receiving Condition:

- You accept that happiness is your natural state. You recognize that when you do not feel happy for a time it is an indication that something you believe is getting in the way of your well-being, and there is something for you to heal.
- You no longer question the existence and role of energy and vibration in your home. You know it is real, even if you don't completely understand it.
- You do not place expectations of perfection upon yourself. You accept that your home is a work in progress and that there always will be more work to do. You are able to love your home as it is and enjoy planning improvements at the same time.
- When circumstances challenge you, you don't retreat into drama and worry, at least not for long. You know that change and challenge are a natural part of life, especially at home.
- You are generally kind to yourself and others, especially at home.

- You are in action at home every day without even trying.

Align, trust and allow

Even though disciplined action can be required at times, a powerful component of living in Receiving Condition is learning to align the energy to what you want, trust, and allow the Universe to deliver in perfect time. When you release the need to control exactly how and when things happen, you open yourself to new possibilities, often much better than those you were hoping for. Your home gives you the perfect place to practice aligning, allowing and trusting—whether with backsplash tile, front steps, art, or even a tea towel.

Sometimes when things appear to be going wrong, they are actually going right but it's just not obvious, yet. I see good examples of this with my husband's real estate clients. Almost always when people are disappointed at not getting a particular house, it ends up being a blessing for them. Sometimes a better home appears in a better location at a better price, the client gets an unexpected new job that allows them to increase their budget or changes their location, or they find out they are going to have a baby, which changes their needs. Trust that everything is in perfect order.

If you believe that you have to "make" good things happen in your life, relax. If you are aware, have asked for what you want, are taking action when needed, you will be fine. Remain open to inspiration, catch resistant thoughts, and be patient. Align, trust, and allow, and have fun seeing what happens. A good practice is to ask the Universe for "this or something better"—and then allow things to flow.

Are you worried about who you will be?

One great question I often hear is, "If I start monitoring my emotions, taking full responsibility for myself at home, and thinking happy, loving thoughts all the time, what will happen to "me"? Who will I be? What will happen to my life as I know it?"

If you are concerned that learning to live consistently from love will somehow make your personality disappear or put your relationships in jeopardy, you can relax. Your personality and your life are safe! It will actually become easier for you to be yourself. You will become more of the beautiful, kind, loving, capable person that you truly are (oh yes, you are!). Your life will likely continue much as it is, only better and easier. If you do make changes in your life as you release resistance, know that the changes will feel right when the time is right. No matter how good it gets, your life will always have its dramas and challenges, but probably fewer dramas and different challenges, and you will know how to deal with them.

You will do just fine.

Chapter Ten
Moving Forward from Here

As you put The 3 Keys into action, and begin to experience and appreciate more and more what it feels like to live in Receiving Condition—perhaps you have experienced changes in your home already—what's next? How do you open the door to your home ever wider, and continue to receive?

Just the beginning

A home in Receiving Condition is your starting point. A home in Receiving Condition is your foundation for having a life that you love in every way. A home in Receiving Condition supports you physically, emotionally, and spiritually to be creative, productive, engaged, and fully your best self in *every* part of your life.

One step at a time

As you change your home, give yourself a chance to shift along with it, and vice versa. Remember, you and your home are energetically connected. If you try to do too much at once, you can risk exhausting yourself and losing momentum.

Just like going up a set of stairs, if you take one step at a time, you will get further in the long run. If you take the steps two at a time, you will go faster for a short spurt, but you will tire more easily and not get as far in the end. If you try to take the steps three at a time, you risk falling flat on your face and hurting yourself. The same is true with shifting things in your home. One step at a time gets you further, faster.

Higher and higher

As you continue to raise your Awareness, you will create new Desire and be moved to even greater Willingness. And so on. As you integrate The 3 Keys into how you live, over time your Awareness, Desire, and Willingness will come to you in deeper layers, like an endless onion, one layer at a time.

Awareness, Desire, and Willingness
↗↗↗
Awareness, Desire, and Willingness
↗↗↗
Awareness, Desire, and Willingness
↗↗↗
Awareness, Desire, and Willingness
↗↗↗
Awareness, Desire, and Willingness

With each shift upward, you will release and heal, and more good things will flow to you. The cycle then begins again, shifting you and your home to higher and higher levels of vibration, allowing you to experience all the benefits that come with that upward shift.

Shifting your vibration to a higher level takes time. If you are making a conscious effort in all of this and still experience periods of feeling stuck, stay with it.

If your Desire is stronger than your Awareness—which is common—you will be frustrated for sure. There are three kinds of Awareness, remember, and Awareness of what you see in your home is just one. Go back and, look again at your color zones and the underlying emotions, examine your thoughts and feelings to see where you are getting blocked. Remind yourself that everything is energy and take action only when it feels good.

If your Awareness (of your home, of your thoughts and feelings, and of how energy works in your home) is at a high level and you are still not experiencing movement in your home, there may be a time of adjustment as you raise your Desire to match your Awareness, and then another time of adjustment as you raise your level of Willingness to match that. Give it time and stay open to inspiration.

Imagine a door with three locks; you need three different keys to open the door to receive: Awareness, Desire, and Willingness, together. If the door isn't opening, go back and see what key is missing, or maybe just needs an adjustment. You will get it.

Embrace new challenges

You will have new challenges at home over time. Embrace them. New challenges are a sign of movement, and affirm your progress as you move to higher levels of Awareness, Desire, and Willingness.

Note: This applies to new challenges when old ones have been resolved. If you have new challenges at home appearing on top of remaining old ones, stop and recognize that there is something there that you need to acknowledge and heal before you can move forward.

Embrace your power

I hope you see by now that you are in charge of your life. Not your spouse, not your family, not your boss, not your government. Others may influence your life, of course, but you are free to choose what you do and what you accept.

Until you truly accept your power, you will experience resistance. When you truly know deep inside you that you shape your life in its essence and details, everything changes.

> *"Do you not see that all of your misery comes from the strange belief that you are powerless?"*
> —*A Course in Miracles*

Enjoy the process

Creating Receiving Condition in your home helps you discover what feels good, natural, right, and beautiful—to you. You will never finish, so let go of the hurry and enjoy.

As you take the time to understand and apply the principles here, you will see that the *heal* in HouseHeal means learning to live from a place of love within you.

HEAL = Home Experienced As Love

If you are willing to work through your beliefs, recognize and change thought patterns that are reflected to you in your home, you will open yourself up to a whole new world.

And you will have so much more to give the world.

> *"Healing oneself is an indispensable piece of the healing of the whole planet."*
> - Rudolph Ballantine, M.D., *Radical Healing*

Learn how to recognize and trust what feels right to *you*. You have within you everything you need to create a home and a life that you love. Learn to be good to yourself. Take your time.

You will need help from lots of people along the way—friends, family, decorators, contractors, energy healers, and many, many more. We are all here to share our talents and gifts and to help each other. But no matter how much help and support you receive from others, you create your own life experience.

Have fun exploring the ever-expanding choices, possibilities, and resources available to you for your home and your life. Above all, be kind to yourself. Give yourself the freedom to say what you really want, from the heart, without fear.

Know that you are safe, you are loved, and you are worthy to receive everything good in life, beginning at home.

About the Author

Sara Brown Crowder, B.A. is a dynamic teacher who helps people to understand the powerful connection between what's in their homes and what's in their lives. Sara's inspiring principle-based teaching opens people up to a whole new world of awareness, and provides them with the practical knowledge and tools to change not only how their home looks and feels, but how their *life* looks and feels. She has spoken at major conferences including the Therapeutic Touch Network of Ontario and The Professional Organizers of Canada. Sara teaches ongoing HouseHeal classes in Toronto, Ontario, Canada, where she lives with her husband, Gary.

To apply the HouseHeal teaching in your daily life:

HouseHeal into Practice

Dear Reader:

What you have read in this book is real, it is powerful, and it works. Still, even if you have taken in everything here with an open mind and an open heart, even if you are inspired and in full-on action at home, there are ever-deeper levels of understanding and practice going forward. Believe me, there are more layers to putting this teaching into practice than you might realize. That is why I offer ongoing courses to support you moving forward, and why I invite you to sign up for a class now, in-person or by teleseminar. Course information, along with access to free resources, is available on my web site at www.househeal.com. I encourage you to have a look and see what might be right for you.

To experience ongoing transformation in your daily life, there is always more personal work to do—*always*, for *all* of us! My HouseHeal students continue to affirm the power of this teaching, and they also eagerly and enthusiastically affirm the need for ongoing support. You in are in charge of your own life and at the same time, you cannot do this alone—we *all* need help from each other! That's what makes life fun! If you are willing to continue to learn and grow, and welcome support, you will experience the greatest, most wonderful changes in your home and in your life!

I look forward to meeting you soon, hearing from you and sharing this beautiful, magical time with you.

With love,

Resources

HouseHeal into Practice

Putting HouseHeal into practice is easier when you have support. To find out about HouseHeal classes, teleseminars, discussions groups, special events with Sara, and additional resources go to www.househeal.com

Sign up for FREE weekly HouseHeal tips and inspiration at www.househeal.com.

To book Sara to speak at your event:
info@househeal.com

To order additional copies of this book:
www.househeal.com

CPSIA information can be obtained at www.ICGtesting.com
Printed in the USA
LVOW120446170413

329463LV00002B/9/P